CREATED FOR
GREATNESS

Living Your Best Life

Through God's Word

CREATED FOR
GREATNESS

Living Your Best Life

Through God's Word

GREG
STEPHENS

BEAVER'S POND PRESS
Saint Paul, Minnesota

Edited by Angela Wiechmann and Gail Glover
Production editor: Hanna Kjeldbjerg

ISBN: 978-1-64343-958-7
Library of Congress Catalog Number: 2019906465
Printed in the United States of America
First Printing: 2020
24 23 22 21 20   5 4 3 2 1

Book design and typesetting by Athena Currier
Select graphics from Vecteezy.com
Typeface: Adobe Garamond Pro

 Beaver's Pond Press
939 Seventh Street West
Saint Paul, MN 55102

(952) 829-8818
www.BeaversPondPress.com

To order, visit www.ItascaBooks.com.

Contact Greg Stephens at www.EquipYourFamily.com for speaking engagements, book club discussions, and interviews.

This book of the law shall not depart out of your mouth, but you shall meditate on it day and night, that you may be careful to do according to all that is written in it; for then you shall make your way prosperous, and then you shall have good success.

—*Joshua 1:8, RSV*

I dedicate this book to my wife, Mary, who is our family's prayer warrior. I treasure her love, support, and encouragement.

My editors, Angie Wiechmann and Gail Glover, and my designer, Athena Currier, are the greatest.

And my faithful family and friends provided helpful insight, guidance, and information for my book: Mary Stephens, David Stephens, Jane Kramer, Garrett Kramer, Anthony Novotne, Shannon Novotne, Cheryl Nelson, Paul Wolner, Amy Sleper, Bill Hart, and Wally Kolsrud.

CONTENTS

AUTHOR'S NOTE

When I was in elementary school, my dad revealed a foolish thing he had done when he was my age. But he immediately followed his admission with this statement: "Do as I say, not as I do." Dad soon realized, however, that his children followed his behavior more than his words.

In fact, before we entered high school, Dad told us an even more important statement: "Your actions speak so loudly that I can't hear what you say." Stated another way, if you don't practice what you preach, people will ignore what you say. This is true for parents—and everyone else.

Years later, I met with a group of executives to explore how to apply God's Word to their business and personal lives. I suddenly remembered Dad's advice as we discussed the importance of teaching God's Word to our children so it would guide and bless their lives. At that point, I remembered that if I wanted my children to listen to me, not only did I have to learn God's Word and apply it to my life, but I also had to model the type of behavior that demonstrated what I preached.

After our meetings concluded, I continued reading and studying God's Word. During my study time, I identified ten life-changing skills that will put an individual in the best possible position to live a happy, successful, and significant life. I then developed a simple format to share these skills with others so they could learn how to apply them to their lives.

Using this simple format, I first met with two family members every Wednesday night for three months, exploring the ten life-changing skills. Then over the course of two years, I met individually with an attorney and a businessman. I also met individually with a college student, an MBA graduate, and a law student.

After these sessions, all the participants suggested I write a book so more people could learn and benefit from these skills. As a result of their encouragement, I agreed.

But before I even typed my first outline, I pored over the twenty large three-ring notebooks that contained thirty-six years' worth of material I'd gathered from God's Word, authors, speakers, ministers, teachers, mentors, and Christian organizations. I had gleaned so much from so many sources. After decades of synthesizing all this material, I realized it would be difficult to write this book in the typical nonfiction fashion.

Consequently, I decided to write the book in a fictional format. The story focuses on a father who shares the ten life-changing skills with his adult son. Although this narrative element is fictional, the anecdotes and examples are straight from my own life experiences.

My hope too is that the fictional format is a welcoming, relatable way for you to engage with the book. Please put yourself in the son's shoes as he takes this life-changing journey. These ten life-changing skills will put you in the best possible position to live a happy, successful, and significant life.

And if you are a parent, my hope is that you can learn these ten life-changing skills so you can then model and teach them to your children. God and His Word will guide and bless their lives, and you will leave a legacy that will contribute to the happiness and success of future generations.

Note: Before I discuss the ten life-changing skills, I want to address two statements I often hear about the Bible. Many people say the Old Testament is just that—old and therefore no longer relevant. Many people also say that the Bible was written by people who either created their own story or interpreted what they saw.

But God's Word tells us that both statements are wrong.

God's Word, as contained in both the Old and New Testament, teaches us what is right, what is wrong, and how to live our lives. Specifically, God's Word says, *"All scripture* is inspired by God and profitable for teaching, for reproof, for correction, and for training in righteousness" (2 Timothy 3:16, RSV emphasis added).

Even though several Biblical authors were eyewitnesses, the words they and the other authors wrote down (referred to as prophecy) did not come from their own interpretation or creative thinking. Rather, the words came from the Holy Spirit, who inspired what they wrote.

Specifically, God's Word says, " . . . no prophecy of scripture is a matter of one's own interpretation, because no prophecy ever came by the impulse of man, but men moved by the Holy Spirit spoke from God" (2 Peter 1:20–21, RSV). Because God inspired the authors, we can trust that their writings are true. Jesus also tells us God's Word is true. He said, "Sanctify them in the truth; thy word is truth" (John 17:17, RSV).

Some people believe that one should not quote God's Word to prove the reliability of the Bible. If you concur, I recommend that you also examine the outside evidence that supports and proves God's Word. Not sure where to start? You can Google your questions and examine the contents on websites such as Focus on the Family.

You can also read books written by brilliant men who started out as skeptics and atheists but became believers. These men engaged in an exhaustive study of manuscript evidence, archeological discoveries, fulfilled prophecies, the Dead Sea Scrolls, the Roman historians, and transformed lives. Afterward, they concluded that the Bible is historically accurate, reliable, and relevant. Here are just three examples of the men and the books they wrote: C. S. Lewis (*Mere Christianity* and *Surprised by Joy*), Josh McDowell (*Evidence That Demands a Verdict* and *The Unshakable Truth*), and Lee Strobel (*The Case for Faith* and *The Case for Christ*).

COMING HOME

Mom calls. Dad's health is declining, and she's worried. I've been meaning to visit for a while, but did I wait too long? To make matters worse, I only have time for a quick visit before heading back home. I'm feeling anxious and a little guilty. I should have come by sooner to see how he was doing.

Plus, there's something I want to ask Dad, something really important I should have asked a long time ago. Will he still be up for it?

As I approach the long, winding driveway to my parents' home, I reflect on my precollege years. Dad always maintained such a good balance between working and spending time with our family. Even though he was a successful executive who labored under time pressures and deadlines, Dad never missed any of my school performances. I always felt as if Dad spelled love *T-I-M-E* because he spent both quantity and quality time with our family.

I was lucky to get to be around some of my Dad's work colleagues when I was little. I remember overhearing a member of Dad's management team comment to a fellow member that he could not understand how Dad accomplished so much work each day and was still able to spend time with his family. I even remember a former partner, who left the firm to start his own business, telling me that one day he hoped he too would be remembered as a family man and a successful leader who made everyone feel valued in the way that my dad did.

Next, I think about the fun times my brother, sister, and I had spent with Dad. Because Dad enjoyed reading and studying the Bible, he never missed a teachable moment to use everyday experiences to share a truth from God's Word. He made these truths come to life because he showed us how they applied right in that moment we were living.

Finally, I think about when we kids were in high school. Dad offered to meet with us once a week during the summer months to discuss ten life-changing skills based on God's Word. Dad learned the skills reading and studying the Bible during the last thirty-six years of his forty-three years as a successful executive.

During this time, he also participated in a group of Bible scholars and business executives that met specifically to discuss life skills they could share with their families. Dad told us that if we chose to learn and apply these skills on a daily basis, they would put us in the best possible position to enjoy a happy, successful, and significant life.

My sister and brother did meet with Dad, but I declined his invitation. I thought I had things pretty well in hand and didn't need any extra help. Looking back, I realize I made a mistake. Since I've left home, things have not gone that well. Even now, I am between jobs. I can't help but feel lost in many ways.

My sister and brother, on the other hand, seem to have benefited from those meetings with Dad. Granted, they have had to deal with their share of problems over the years, but they always seem to recover from them quickly and don't seem so distressed when things don't go as planned. I often wonder what Dad had taught them.

It's time to find out for myself.

As I approach the garage doors, I can see Dad standing at the living room window, peeking out between the curtains. When I walk in, I'm surprised to see that he looks a little pale and somewhat thinner. But after Dad flashes his winning smile and gives me a strong hug, I feel better.

Mom of course swoops in for a hug too. "It's great to see you, dear."

"You too, Mom," I say. I then lean in to whisper, "Mind if I have some time with Dad?"

She nods and smiles, her eyes shiny with tears. "Of course. I'll let you boys be." She squeezes my hand before heading into the living room.

I turn to Dad, but first I take a second to fight back tears of my own. "I'm sorry I didn't come to visit sooner. How are you doing?"

"I'm doing well enough." He smiles and waits.

I take a deep breath. "Dad, I think I need your help. Remember back when you offered to meet with us kids to discuss those life-changing skills?"

"I sure do," he replies. "I always hoped that one day you too would want to learn them, as your brother and sister did."

His encouragement instantly makes me feel relieved. "Well, that's really why I'm here. I do want to learn those skills. Things aren't going so well, and I feel kind of lost. I want to be a happier person. I want to do better at my work. I want to learn those skills to model them in my life and teach them to my family. But I don't know how to do it. You always seem to know how to handle situations. Would you teach me? Would that be OK with you?"

"Of course!" He flashes that smile again and gives me another hug.

I can feel the tension lift a little from my shoulders for a moment, but then it returns.

"The only thing is . . . I know you usually do these lessons in person, but I have to head back home. I'm in the middle of sending résumés and scheduling interviews and—well, you get the picture. I really want to do this work with you, but I don't know how."

Dad gives me a reassuring pat on the shoulder. "No problem. Over the years, I've written out all this information. Who knows, maybe it could be a book someday." He chuckles. "I can mail you letters for each of the ten skills."

My mouth turns in a playful smirk. "Great, but how about you just *email* them instead? You do have them as Word files, right? Please tell me these aren't from that ancient typewriter you used to have."

Dad gives a hearty laugh. "Of course, I can email them! Though for fun, let me show you what some of the original drafts look like," he adds with a wink. "Why don't you head in to make us some tea while I run and get them."

As Dad heads to his office, I head to the kitchen to put on the teapot. When he returns, he's holding a thick three-ring notebook that's all but bursting with pages. While the water heats up, we chat about the weather and the latest win of our favorite team.

Once we each get a cup of tea, we sit down at the kitchen table. I can see out the window that the sun's trying to come out. The house is very quiet.

Dad breaks the silence. His voice is steady and reassuring.

"Before we get started on this process, I think it is important for you to know something about me and my experiences. You mentioned that I always seemed to know what to do. That wasn't always the case. Things changed for me when I became a believer. Even though I am confident that you are a believer, I would still like to share my path of learning. I was very fortunate to have a mentor who guided me many years ago in how to become a believer."

Then Dad says something that surprises me.

"I didn't become a believer until my midthirties."

I sit back in my chair. Considering how strong Dad is in his faith, I'd always assumed he'd been a believer all his life. This is why his revelation strikes me. For some reason, it makes me feel even more relaxed. Maybe Dad's path wasn't so different from my own after all.

Dad silently smiles at my reaction before continuing. "I knew I was missing something in my life and didn't quite know what it was or what to do about it. I thought that having some-one to help me figure things out would make it a little easier. I started asking around for someone that I could meet with, and I was connected with Martin through a friend. Until then, I did not realize that I had a problem with God. But my mentor Martin carefully explained to me what my problem was and how to fix it."

Dad pauses. "But that's my journey. For now, though, let's talk about this journey you're about to begin." His eyes light up with excitement as he pats the notebook in front of him.

I listen intently as Dad goes on to explain how we'll focus on ten life-changing skills based on God's Word. He says they take some time to learn, because they require not only new habits but a new way of thinking and viewing life while we live it. He reminds me of God's truths he shared with us when we were little and how we learned over time. This makes me smile, because I had just been thinking of them myself. He then reassures me that I can learn these skills but that I will need diligence and will also need to be patient with myself through the process.

"Wow," I say. "This sounds great. Now I understand why that notebook is so full. You really do have a lot of material about these ten skills."

Dad lets out a snort. "Are you kidding? This is just one of *twenty* notebooks."

My mouth drops open. I suddenly feel like an incoming freshman seeing a college syllabus for the first time. This will be quite the education!

Dad opens to a page featuring a handwritten list of the ten skills. He turns it toward me. "I have the skills numbered, but you can go in any order. So which one of these skills would you like to start with, son?"

1. Finding lasting happiness.
2. Ensuring peak performance.
3. Maintaining a positive attitude.
4. Creating and maintaining balance.
5. Setting and achieving goals.
6. Making better decisions.
7. Managing problems.
8. Managing worry, fear, anxiety, and stress.
9. Managing time.
10. Creating and maintaining a powerful prayer life.

I slump back in my chair. I truly want to learn—and embrace—all these skills. But it doesn't seem possible.

"Dad, I have to be honest, I'm a little overwhelmed. I don't know where to start. I can't see how I can do any of this, actually."

Dad smiles and says, "It's always hard to know where and how to start. The important thing is to just take that first step. What does your heart tell you?"

I study the list again, trying to set aside my fears. "I don't know . . . I guess if I could just feel happy most of the time, that would be great. So, maybe 'Finding lasting happiness' is the one that feels most right to me. And you do have it listed as number one here, so it just makes sense."

Dad nods. "You made an excellent choice, son. Everyone wants to be happy."

With that, Dad stretches in his chair and cringes a little with pain. He pauses for a moment, then nods, almost to himself.

"You know, this emailing idea might work best for me too. To be honest, I don't know if I could make it through those long in-person sessions anymore. I'm moving a bit slower these days. In fact, I'm feeling a little tired now, so I think I might retire early. Maybe you can visit with your mother before you head out."

Swallowing back the lump in my throat, I help him to his feet.

"Now," he says, wagging a finger at me, "you have some homework to do. I want you to think about how you would answer these two questions: First, what makes you happy, and does it last? Second, where do you think lasting happiness comes from? Happiness and *happiness that lasts* can be two different things, and it is important to know that difference. Be sure to spend some time with those questions tonight. I'll send your first email bright and early tomorrow."

"Will do," I say.

We hug again.

"Thank you for coming, son. I'm so happy you're ready to take this journey."

"Speaking of journeys . . ." I begin. "Could you someday tell me about your journey to becoming a believer? I'd love to hear that story."

Dad thinks for a moment, his eyes moving toward his notebook. "Actually, I have just the thing. Watch your inbox," he adds with a wink.

After Dad retires for the evening, Mom and I visit for an hour. We haven't talked for a while, and she wants to know how the job search is going. She asks about the kids and my wife and how we're all coping with the stress of me being without a job. She listens intently.

Then I finally say, "So, Mom, how is Dad really doing?"

She doesn't say anything for a moment, then looks me in the eye. "Not so great. He gets tired easily and actually takes naps now. He never used to do that. We don't know much right now, but we'll keep you posted. Your visit meant a lot to him. Thank you."

Her eyes are dry this time. She knows it's hard for me to hear this, and I appreciate that she doesn't make it harder by bringing her own emotions into the message. She always somehow knows when it's the right time to do that.

I nod. "Thanks for letting me know that, Mom."

It's getting late, and I have a long drive. So we hug and say our goodbyes, then I slowly drive out the driveway.

On the way home, my phone beeps. There's an email. I know it's from Dad. It's the story about how he became a believer.

I look down at my gas gauge. I have more than a half tank left, but I decide to turn into a gas station anyway. I quickly pump my gas, then I pull into a parking space to open Dad's email.

Dear Son,

The ten life-changing skills show *believers* how to live their life through God's Word. And even though I am confident you are a believer, I would still like to share the story of how I became a believer.

As I said today, I didn't become a believer until my midthirties. Until then, I did not realize I had a problem with God that I needed to fix.

Thankfully, my mentor Martin carefully explained what that problem was and how to fix it. He began by telling me that my sins had created a separation between God and me (Isaiah 59:2).

"Well," I replied, "sin may cause separation for *some* people, but not for me."

I did not consider myself a "sinner." I was a good person. I wasn't perfect, but I was definitely not as bad as some people I knew.

"When it comes to sin," Martin said, "the comparison is not between you and another person, but rather between you and God."

As Martin explained, each and every one of us is a sinner. God's Word tells us, "since *all* have sinned and fall short of the glory of God" (Romans 3:23, emphasis added).

"OK," I said. "I admit I may have committed a few minor sins. But so what?"

Martin went on to tell me that my "so-what sins" had resulted in death. God's Word tells us that "the wages of sin is death" (Romans 6:23). That is the consequence.

Obviously, this news was not encouraging. Sensing my concern, Martin told me that there was good news.

Namely, Christ had died for me in order to pay the penalty for my sins.

Specifically, God's Word says, "But God shows his love for us in that while we were yet sinners Christ died for us" (Romans 5:8, RSV). His Word also says, "For Christ also died for sins once for all, the righteous for the unrighteous, that he might bring us to God, being put to death in the flesh but made alive in the spirit" (1 Peter 3:18, RSV).

I thought I was pretty smart, so I asked Martin one question: "Does God love me?" After he answered yes, I followed that up with one statement: "Surely a loving God would never send someone He loved to a place where they would be forever separated from His presence."

"Where you end up for eternity is your choice," Martin answered. "But because God loves you, He sent His own Son, Jesus, to pay the penalty for your sins. If you accept His love and the fact that Jesus had paid the penalty for your sins, you can be with Him for eternity. But if you reject His love and what Jesus has done for you on the cross, you will be forever separated from Him. The choice is yours. And if you decide to make no choice, that's the same as making a choice to reject what God and Jesus have done for you."

"Surely there must be someone other than Jesus who can close the divide my sins have created between God and me," I said. Actually, I was still looking for a way to escape a decision.

"No," Martin answered. "Jesus is the only way."

He then quoted Acts 4:12 (RSV), which states, "And there is salvation in no one else, for there is no other name under heaven given among men by which we must be saved." Furthermore, God's Word tells us in 1 Timothy 2:5–6 (RSV), "For there is one God, and there is one mediator between God and men, the man Christ Jesus, who gave himself as a ransom for all, the testimony to which was borne at the proper time."

In addition, Jesus said, " . . . I am the way, and the truth, and the life; no one comes to the Father, but by me" (John 14:6, RSV). As Martin explained, Jesus did not say He was *a* truth. No, Jesus said He was *the* truth. Martin also pointed out that Jesus did not say that there were *many* ways to come to God. Instead, Jesus said he was *the only* way.

I then asked Martin, "If Jesus is the only way to God, what—if anything—do I have to do in order to gain access to Jesus?"

To answer my question, Martin quoted Revelation 3:20, where Jesus tells us that He stands at the door of our heart and knocks, and if we open the door, he will come into our life. Therefore, Martin was saying that I had to open the door to my heart and receive Jesus. In fact, if we want to become children of God, we must receive Him. John 1:12 (RSV) says, "But to all who received him, who believed in his name, he gave power to become children of God."

"So, all I have to do is 'believe' in order to be saved?" I asked.

Martin said, "Most scholars agree that the Greek and Hebrew words for *believe* actually mean 'receive.' So to believe Jesus is to receive Jesus."

Martin then used a simple analogy to help me understand the difference between *believe* and *receive*. If I have a headache, I may believe that a pain pill will cure it. But my belief in the pill won't do any good unless I actually receive it by swallowing it.

Similarly, I could believe that Jesus is God's Son. But my simple belief doesn't do any good unless I actually receive Him into my life as Lord and Savior. In fact, the Bible says that even the demons believe Jesus is God's Son (James

2:19)—and everyone knows that Jesus is *not* the demons' Lord and Savior.

"So all I need to do is receive Jesus in order to be saved for eternity?" I asked. "Really? That's it? I thought I had to perform a sufficient number of good works."

"You are not saved by good works," Martin replied.

He went on to explain that in Ephesians 2:8–9 (RSV), God's Word tells us, "For by grace you have been saved through faith; and this is not your own doing, it is the gift of God—not because of works, lest any man should boast."

Martin next shared verses from the Bible that specifically guaranteed me eternal life:

- "For God so loved the world that he gave his only Son, that whoever believes in him should not perish but have eternal life." (John 3:16, RSV)

- "Jesus said to her, I am the resurrection and the life; he who believes in me, though he die, yet shall he live, and whoever lives and believes in me shall never die . . . " (John 11:25–26, RSV)

- "because, if you confess with your lips that Jesus is Lord and believe in your heart that God raised him from the dead, you will be saved." (Romans 10:9, RSV)

- "And this is the testimony, that God gave us eternal life, and this life is in his Son. He who has the Son has life; he who has not the Son of God has not life. I write this to you who believe in the name of the Son of God, that you may know that you have eternal life." (1 John 5:11–13, RSV)

Martin summarized these key verses in an illustration that clearly shows how Jesus is the bridge between me and God:

THE BRIDGE BETWEEN MAN AND GOD

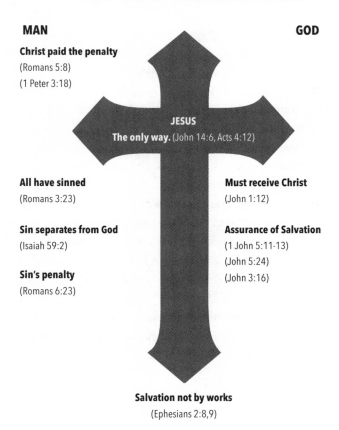

MAN

GOD

Christ paid the penalty
(Romans 5:8)
(1 Peter 3:18)

JESUS
The only way. (John 14:6, Acts 4:12)

All have sinned
(Romans 3:23)

Must receive Christ
(John 1:12)

Sin separates from God
(Isaiah 59:2)

Assurance of Salvation
(1 John 5:11-13)
(John 5:24)

Sin's penalty
(Romans 6:23)

(John 3:16)

Salvation not by works
(Ephesians 2:8,9)

"Asking for and receiving salvation is a decision of the heart," Martin said. "So what do you really believe in your heart? In 1 Samuel 16:7, God's Word says that man looks on the outward appearance, but God looks on the heart. Only God knows your heart. But do not play games with God, because God is not mocked, as we learn in Galatians 6:7."

Martin then told me the story about one of the thieves hanging on the cross next to Jesus. In verses 40–43 of Luke 23, the thief acknowledged his wrongdoing and asked Jesus to remember him when He came into His kingdom. Jesus, knowing the man's heart, responded by telling the repentant thief that today he would be with Him in paradise. In fact, God's Word tells us, "For, 'every one who calls upon the name of the Lord will be saved'" (Romans 10:13, RSV).

Martin ended his counsel on how to receive salvation: "You must admit that you need salvation, because you are a sinner. You must repent by turning away from your sins. You must believe that Jesus died for your sins and that God raised Him from the grave. And you must ask Jesus to come into your life as Lord and Savior."

Then he gave me one example of a simple prayer: "Dear Jesus, I believe You died to pay the penalty for my sins, and then God raised You from the dead. I am asking You for forgiveness and for You to come into my life as my Lord and Savior. Amen."

I became a believer that day. I received Jesus as my Lord and Savior.

This is what it means to be a believer. And as believers, we know we are created for greatness when we live by God's Word.

It takes me a while to realize I have tears in my eyes. Dad's journey to faith fills me with hope.

Ten life-changing skills. Here we go.

CHAPTER ONE
FINDING LASTING HAPPINESS

Bright and early the next morning, before my alarm has even gone off, my cell phone beeps. I have an incoming email. Sure enough, it's from Dad—the first letter and the first life-changing skill. Once again, I'm surprised by how excited I am to open it.

But then I sheepishly realize I haven't done my "homework," as he had asked. I decide to buy some time by hopping in the shower.

Standing there in the warm water, I think about what makes me happy. I'm happy when I spend time with my wife and kids. I'm also happy when reading a good book or exercising. However, I have to admit that my happiness tends to ebb and flow, depending on what I'm doing at any given moment. For instance, it's often hard to feel happy when submitting resume after resume.

When we were growing up, Dad always stressed the importance of involving God in our daily lives if we wanted to be happy. But now I'm not so sure I know what that means. I'm not even sure if I know what this kind of happiness is, what it feels like, or how to keep it. Suddenly, I feel pretty discouraged about my chances of living a life of *ongoing* happiness, as Dad described.

19

As I climb out of the shower, I remember that Dad also told us that there is one God in three Divine Persons. God, the Father, is our creator (Isaiah 64:8). Jesus, the Son, came to earth in bodily form "to seek and to save the lost" (Luke 19:10). Finally, the Holy Spirit is the counselor (John 14:16) who helps us pray (Romans 8:26) and understand spiritual truth (1 Corinthians 2:10–14). Just thinking about that somehow makes me feel better.

I dress, make a cup of coffee, then settle at my desk. Taking a deep breath, I open the letter from Dad.

I'm ready to learn.

Dear Son,

Your grandfather always said that having knowledge without applying it to improve your life was a waste. So I'll not only share the principles to finding lasting happiness, but I will also show you how to apply them to your everyday life.

Everyone everywhere wants to be happy. The international community even set aside March 20 of every year as the International Day of Happiness!

The pursuit of happiness is even in the United States Declaration of Independence as a right. It states in part, "We hold these truths to be self-evident, that all men are created equal, that they are endowed by their Creator with certain unalienable Rights, that among these are Life, Liberty and the *pursuit of Happiness*" (emphasis added).

There are two types of happiness. One type is temporary. The other type is lasting.

Different things bring temporary happiness to different people. What makes one person temporarily happy may not be the same for another person. There is no one "source."

Think about what provides that kind of happiness for you. Perhaps it's watching your favorite TV show, playing golf with a friend, or going out to dinner as a family.

It might help to make a list of people, things, and activities that bring you that feeling of happiness. Be sure to schedule time each day to enjoy at least one of them.

It's important, though, not to limit your definition of happiness to these short-term situations and fleeting moments. True happiness—lasting happiness—is a constant state of inner peace. Some people might think of it in terms of the word *joy*.

Even though there is no single source of temporary happiness, there *is* one source of lasting happiness: God.

God did not create us to have a smiley face twenty-four seven. After all, even Jesus wept (John 11:35). But He did send His Son, Jesus, to earth so that we may enjoy an abundant life (John 10:10). And the abundant life includes lasting happiness.

So, how do we achieve this lasting happiness that comes from God? By "feeding" our body, soul, and spirit with the right "food." And by living the way that God created us to live.

FEEDING OUR BODY, SOUL, AND SPIRIT

As we know, there is one God in three Divine Persons—The Father, the Son, and the Holy Spirit. And every human person has three components—the body, the soul, and the spirit.

Bible scholars agree that we have a body that houses our soul and spirit. Paul recognized our three-part makeup when he said, "May the God of peace himself sanctify you wholly; and may your *spirit* and *soul* and *body* be kept sound and blameless at the coming of our Lord Jesus Christ" (1 Thessalonians 5:23, RSV, emphasis added).

Paul—or possibly another author of the book of Hebrews—further confirmed that each person is composed of a soul, spirit, and body when he said, "For the word of God is living and active, sharper than any two-edged sword, piercing to the division of *soul* and *spirit*, of joints and marrow [*body*], and discerning the thoughts and intentions of the heart" (Hebrews 4:12, RSV, emphasis added).

In order to maintain lasting happiness, we must therefore satisfy not only our body but also our soul and spirit with nourishing "food."

Let's look at each aspect more closely.

Body

A person's body is what we see. If you want to put yourself in the best possible position to enjoy lasting happiness, you must eat healthy food, engage in regular exercise, and get sufficient sleep.

But there's much more, because part of our body is our mind. God's Word tells us to guard our mind because our life flows from our thoughts (Proverbs 4:23; 23:7).

Most of us have heard the phrase "garbage in, garbage out." Maybe that phrase derived from Luke 6:45: "The good man out of the good treasure of his heart produces good, and the evil man out of his evil treasure produces evil; for out of the abundance of the heart his mouth speaks."

Whatever the source of the phrase, we know we need to prevent garbage from entering our mind. When I first became a believer, I put a rubber band around my wrist. Whenever I thought garbage thoughts, including negative thoughts, I snapped myself with the rubber band. Boy, did I have a swollen wrist. (Your mom may tell you that there are days when I should put the rubber band back on my wrist. And she would be right!)

Another good way to keep garbage out is to be transformed by the renewal of our mind (Romans 12:2). We can achieve this renewal by thinking about what is true. That is, we can think about Jesus, who is truth (John 14:6), and about God's Word, which is truth (John 17:17).

Soul

Our soul is that part of us that experiences love and anger as well as peace and anxiety. If you are like me, you spend time and money to improve your body and physical life. But how much time and money do you spend to improve your soul?

Your soul is more valuable than anything in this world. It is eternal, which means it will either spend eternity with God or be separated from Him.

Jesus even said, "For what shall it profit a man, if he shall gain the whole world, and lose his own soul?" (Mark 8:36 KJV). Your soul is so important that Jesus also said, "And do not fear those who kill the body but cannot kill the soul; rather fear him who can destroy both soul and body in hell" (Matthew 10:28, RSV).

When your soul is unhappy, you feel irritable, anxious, or bored. More importantly, you feel empty. You feel a void, an inner hunger that prevents you from experiencing lasting happiness.

Many people don't know how to truly feed their soul. As a result, they try to fill that spiritual void with nonspiritual things, such as secular activities, purchases, and pleasures. It's a futile pursuit.

For instance, some people try to fill the void with the best car, the best clothes, and the best vacations. A few have even adopted the saying: "He who dies with the most toys wins."

I admit I fell into the same trap when I was younger. I thought I could maintain my happiness if I just had more money, so I could buy whatever I wanted. I thought that would take away the feeling that something was missing in my life. So, I developed a hunger and thirst for more money, more of everything.

But "more" did not satisfy my soul's hunger and thirst.

When I told my mentor Martin about my problem, he told me to read John 4:13–14 (RSV), where Jesus said, "Every one who drinks of this water will thirst again, but whoever drinks of the water that I shall give him will never thirst."

Why? Because the hunger and thirst I experienced was a spiritual hunger. Only God, Jesus, the Holy Spirit, and God's Word can satisfy a hungry and thirsty soul.

Martin also told me to read John 6:35 (RSV), where Jesus said, "I am the bread of life; he who comes to me shall not hunger, and he who believes in me shall never thirst." In other words, if we want to satisfy our hungry and thirsty soul, we need to spend daily time with God by worshiping Him, praying, reading the Bible, meditating on His Word, and applying it to our life.

Our soul thirsts for the living God (Psalm 63:1; 143:6), and our soul finds rest in God alone (Psalm 62:1, 5). In fact, St. Augustine once said about God, "You have made us for yourself, and our souls are restless until they find rest in you." Note that God's Word does not say that our soul finds rest in our bank account or stock portfolio.

Here's an easy way to remember to feed your soul every day: whenever you feed your body, take time to feed your soul as well. That is, whenever you eat food, feed your soul at the same time through fellowship with God. That includes praying to Him, reading His Word, and applying it to your life.

Spirit

Our spirit is our true being. In the book of Job, God's Word tells us, "But it is the spirit in a man, the breath of the Almighty, that makes him understand . . . " (Job 32:8, RSV). Our spirit is different from the Holy Spirit. Rather, God gave us our spirit to have fellowship with Him and the Holy Spirit. Paul tells us, "it is the Spirit himself bearing witness with our spirit that we are children of God" (Romans 8:16, RSV).

Many Bible scholars believe that our conscience is part of our inner spirit. God uses our conscience to provide us with the basis for making the right decisions. Paul said that he always did his best to have a clear conscience before God and before men (Acts 24:16).

Before we act, our conscience attempts to tell us whether our contemplated action is right or wrong. Therefore, when your conscience speaks to you, you should examine it based on God's Word rather than on society's word.

Like your soul, your spirit is eternal. It is important, then, to feed your spirit on a daily basis to keep it healthy and happy. Even though our soul and spirit are different, they both require the same type of "food."

Therefore, feed your spirit with the same spiritual food you feed your soul. Every day, set aside time to worship God, pray, read the Bible, meditate on His Word, and apply it to your life. Again, a good time to practice this is whenever you eat and feed your body.

As you can see, mealtime is truly the best time to nourish your whole self—body, soul, and spirit—with God's source of lasting happiness.

LIVING AS GOD CREATED US TO LIVE

The second prong to achieving lasting happiness is by living as God intends us to live. As I learned from my mentor Martin as well as from a leader in the Navigators, a large Christian organization, God provides us five purposes and five callings.

My personal experience, and the experiences of several people I know, confirms that when we do what God created us to do (His purposes), we are the happiest. The five purposes, then, are the reasons why God created us. The five callings represent an action course God provides us so we may carry out His purposes.

Stated another way, we are best able to carry out God's five purposes for our life when we follow His five callings. If we want to be physically and emotionally better equipped to accomplish God's five purposes, we must follow the five callings.

Let me share these insights with you, as my mentors shared them with me.

God's Five Purposes

Again, these are the reasons why God created us. If we live out these purposes, we will be living the way God intended us to live.

1. **The Great Commandment: Love God with all your heart, soul, and mind (Matthew 22:37).**

God's Word tells us to make love our aim (1 Corinthians 14:1). When we love someone, we want to spend time with them. And when we spend time with them, we are happier.

Let me ask you, then: Do you love God? If so, how much daily time do you spend with him?

I had a friend who spent no time with God. In fact, he thought that he could be happy apart from God. He bought a beautiful lake home and a new BMW. One day, he told me he was so happy—his life couldn't get any better. But then six months later, he confided in me that his happiness had faded. He couldn't understand why.

Why is it that with all our material wealth, we often feel unhappy? Could it be that we have misidentified what brings lasting happiness?

When you were growing up, I often told you kids to learn from the mistakes of others, because you can't live long enough to make all the mistakes yourself. So when it comes to learning from other's mistakes, one person we can look to is King Solomon. He wrote the book of Ecclesiastes to keep us from wasting our time pursuing happiness in all the wrong places.

Although Solomon was the richest man who had ever lived, he was unable to find lasting happiness. I often wondered why. After all, David, Solomon's father, understood that we find lasting happiness when we are in the presence of God (Psalm 16:11). I'm confident that David shared this wisdom with Solomon. Nevertheless, sometimes sons and daughters don't listen to everything their parents tell them, and they end up learning the hard way!

Sure enough, Solomon decided to find the answer on his own. He used his wealth to obtain every type of pleasure. At the end of his journey, though, Solomon concluded that having more of everything does not produce lasting happiness. He said that apart from God, all is vanity and chasing after the wind (Ecclesiastes 1:14). You might consider lasting happiness a "byproduct" of spending time with God (Psalm 16:11).

2. A Similar Commandment: Love your neighbor as yourself (Matthew 22:39).

God's Word tells us to love one another (John 15:17). However, it's important to understand that *love* is an action verb (1 John 3:18). That means we can't just tell someone we love them. We have to demonstrate our love by our actions.

When is the last time you helped or encouraged someone as an action of love?

God created us to do good things for others (Ephesians 2:10)—not just to consume resources and serve ourselves

(Ephesians 4:11–12). Therefore, use some time and resources to do good things for others, such as helping those in need (1 Timothy 6:17–19).

In addition, God wants us to use the gifts He has given us to serve others (1 Peter 4:10; Romans 12:6–8; 1 Corinthians 12:7–11). Do you know what your gifts are? If not, read these verses to identify your gifts, and then use one or more of them to help and encourage others.

3. The New Commandment: Love others as Christ loves you (John 13:34).

God's Word tells us what love is and is not: "Love is patient and kind; love is not jealous or boastful; it is not arrogant or rude. Love does not insist on its own way; it is not irritable or resentful; it does not rejoice at wrong, but rejoices in the right. Love bears all things, believes all things, hopes all things, endures all things" (1 Corinthians 13:4–7, RSV).

Does that describe how you show your love? If not, what is your plan to take corrective action? And remember, love is an action, not an emotion.

4. The Great Commission: Go and make disciples of all nations (Matthew 28:19).

Jesus said that He "came to seek and to save the lost" (Luke 19:10). In turn, God's Word tells us as well to go to His lost sheep (Matthew 10:6) to feed and tend to them (John 21:15–17).

God also tells us to be His witness (Acts 1:8). This means being a witness not just at church, not just at home, but everywhere we go in life.

I must admit, the first time a friend told me I needed to be a witness at work, I protested. I said my job title and my company's policy prevented me from being a witness for Jesus Christ.

But my friend's response returned me to reality. He told me that witnessing is not a statement you make once. It's not even an activity. It's a way of life. Your entire life shows an unbeliever what their life would look like if they decided to make Jesus their Lord and Savior. So whether I liked it or not, every day and everywhere I was either a witness *for* or *against* Christ by my words, deeds, and actions.

And so are you.

5. The Cultural Mandate: Tend to your family and your work (Genesis 1:28; 1 Timothy 5:8).

God's Word provides us a blueprint for how to approach some of the most important areas of our life: our family and our work.

First, we must take care of our family. God's Word even tells us that if we don't provide for our family, we have "disowned the faith" and are "worse than an unbeliever" (1 Timothy 5:8).

Second, God's Word tells a married man to love his wife "as Christ loved the church and gave himself up for her" (Ephesians 5:25, RSV). In turn, God's Word tells a married woman to help her husband (Genesis 2:18), love him (Titus 2:4), respect him (Ephesians 5:33), and voluntarily submit to his servant leadership (Ephesians 5:22).

Many years ago, I gave a presentation on the defense of the gospel to a group of college students. One female student raised her hand. She said that while she understood what the Bible said, she would never submit to any man.

My response was simple: I said that if I were married to her, I would agree to switch roles. She would be the "husband," and I would be the "wife." I would gladly submit to her, as long as she loved me as Christ loved the church, was willing to die for me, and was leading me based only on God's Word.

I told her I would continue being happy as her hypothetical "wife" under those facts. Why? Because neither of us would be submitting to anyone but God. We would both be on the same page, each basing our decisions on God's Word. In fact, God's Word tells us *all* to be subject to one another out of reverence for Christ (Ephesians 5:21).

Third, God's Word tells us to teach our children about God and His Word (Deuteronomy 6:6–7). This includes teaching and instructing our children on how to live (Proverbs 1:8; 22:6).

Might I add that this is why I'm so pleased to share these ten life-changing skills based on God's Word with you. I hope you may someday share them with your own children as well.

Fourth, God's Word tells us to work with enthusiasm and with a commitment to excellence, as if we were working for the Lord and not for men (Colossians 3:23; Ephesians 6:7). Also, God's Word tells us " . . . be steadfast, immovable, always abounding in the work of the Lord, knowing that in the Lord your labor is not in vain (1 Corinthians 15:58, RSV).

Truly, the work of the Lord is to love and serve others and to share the gospel by living a lifestyle that pleases the Lord (1 Thessalonians 2:8). If we do these things, we will continue to be happy.

God's Five Calls
Again, the five callings make up an action course of sorts that allows us to carry out God's five purposes.

1. Seek first His kingdom and His righteousness (Matthew 6:33).

These three are eternal: God, His Word, and people. As we discussed earlier, we will either spend eternity with God or separated from Him. Everything else will perish.

So, how much time and money do you spend on what lasts for eternity versus what will perish?

God wants us to live with an eternal purpose (His kingdom). At the same time, He also wants us to live with an earthly purpose (His righteousness). That means doing what is right and what pleases Him. This includes spending time with Him, reading His Word and applying it to our lives, and loving and serving people.

God also tells us not to store up treasures for ourselves on earth, where thieves can break in and steal. Rather, we should store up treasures in heaven, where they will be safe from thieves (Matthew 6:19–20).

These verses have a special meaning for me. Early in our marriage, your mom and I stored up earthly treasures in our house. When we were both at work one afternoon, burglars broke in and stole jewelry, money, and other items. When I went to my Bible class that evening, something interesting occurred: we studied Matthew 6:19–20. Obviously, God wanted to teach me a lesson!

2. Keep your eyes on Jesus (Hebrews 12:2).

Remember the story of Peter walking on water (Matthew 14:28–30)? As long as Peter kept his eyes on Jesus, he was able to walk on water. However, as soon as he took his eyes off Jesus and looked at the waves and wind, he began to sink. It was a matter of focus.

The waves and wind represented Peter's problems. Many times in life, we all find ourselves focused on the waves and wind as it rages around us. But if we want to enjoy lasting happiness, we must keep our eyes—our focus—on Jesus.

3. Think on what is true, honorable, just, pure, excellent, and worthy of praise (Philippians 4:8).

Just as Peter struggled when he focused on the waves and wind, we struggle when we fill our minds and lives with negativity. God does not want us to focus on toxic thoughts. Instead, God wants us to first identify those negative thoughts and then replace them with positive thoughts. This is similar to the idea of "feeding" our mind with good, healthy "food."

As you think about your life, what is true and pure? What is worthy of praise?

4. Walk with God, do justice, love kindness, lead a life that pleases God, and get to know Him better (Micah 6:8; Colossians 1:10).

God wants us to trust Him. To do this, we must read His Word in order to know Him better.

Once we place our trust in God, we must then show love, kindness, and mercy to others. This means having the courage to do justice—to do the right thing. In fact, God's Word tells us that happy are those who observe justice (Psalm 106:3).

5. Live a holy life in all of your conduct (1 Peter 1:15).

Everyone knows that trying to live a holy life is no easy task. This is why the Holy Spirit dwells inside every believer and gives us power. The Holy Spirit enables believers to do things they could not do on their own.

Therefore, ask the Holy Spirit to provide you with the necessary power to break any bondage to sin. Ask for the power to live a holy life.

FILLING YOUR TANKS

I hope you are beginning to see why lasting happiness can only come from God. And you can achieve this happiness by feeding your body, soul, and spirit with the right "food" and by living the way God created you to live.

But as I mentioned before, God doesn't expect you to wear a smile all day, every day. Life has its ups and downs—it can feel like a roller coaster. It's one thing to know the source of lasting happiness. It's another thing to achieve it and then maintain it. At times, you may find it difficult.

If your happiness starts to subside, there is a way to identify the problem and take corrective action. It's a simple car analogy my mentor Martin shared with me.

Cars are built—created—to run on gas. Everyone knows a car can't run unless there's gas in the tank. And every car has a gas gauge that warns you when your tank is nearly empty. It's important, then, to keep the needle off the *E*.

So think of it this way: God created—built—you to love and serve Him and to love and serve others. You can't "run" unless you do what God created you to do. That is, you can't achieve lasting happiness unless you love and serve God and others. In a way, you have not one but two gas tanks: your spiritual tank and your service tank.

Fortunately, we too have "gauges" that alert us when our tanks are nearly empty. Your happiness is the gauge. When you notice your happiness fade or when it becomes hard to sustain, that means both needles are nearly on *E*.

If you want to maintain your happiness, you need to keep both tanks full. Martin told me that our *spiritual tank* becomes full when we choose to focus on God and receive spiritual food through praying, reading His Word, and applying it to our life. And our *service tank* becomes full when we choose to focus on others and find ways to love and serve them.

Originally, I created a 1.75-inch-by-2.75-inch card that I carried in my billfold. Now I have it on my smartphone. It shows my spiritual tank and my service tank, each with an "indicator" to remind me to check my tanks. Your finished product might look like this:

SPIRITUAL TANK

Turn your mind towards God. (Psalm 16:11)

SERVICE TANK

Turn your mind toward others. (1 Thessalonians 2:8)

If you feel your happiness starting to subside, read the card. It will help you identify the issue: your spiritual tank and your service tank are either empty or nearly empty.

The card will also help you take corrective action. You can refill your spiritual tank by focusing on God and refill your service tank by focusing on others. After you refill your tanks, happiness will return. And if you continue to keep both tanks full, you will be able to enjoy lasting happiness.

THE ONE THING

In this letter, we covered a lot of material about finding and maintaining happiness that lasts. I'm sure your mind is spinning with ideas, and I'm sure you're excited to implement them all. Then again, maybe all these ideas have left you unsure where to start.

The best way to change your life is one small step at a time. First you take one step, then another. So instead of trying to implement everything you've learned, or instead of feeling so overwhelmed that you don't implement anything, just ask yourself this question: What is *one thing* I can do to help me achieve and maintain my happiness?

For example, maybe you will decide the one thing that you can do is make the card that reminds you to keep your spiritual tank and your service tank full and put it on your smartphone. After you develop a habit of monitoring your spiritual tank and your service tank and keeping them full, you can then identify and act on the next "one thing."

It's a process. Just know I'm here to support you through each step, son.

Love,

Dad

I slowly lean back in my chair. For a long moment, I'm still. Then I let out a deep breath.

What a letter. What a gift this is from Dad.

He's right, though—my mind is spinning with all the wonderful things he had shared about lasting happiness. I appreciate his "one thing" concept. That does seem like a smart way to approach it all.

I really like the idea of making a card to remind me to keep my two tanks full and putting it on my smartphone. It's true that life feels like a roller coaster, and my happiness goes up and down with it.

At that moment, I pick up my phone and call Dad.

"Good morning," he greets me. "Did you get a chance to read the letter yet?"

"I sure did," I reply. "It's . . . it's amazing."

I can practically see Dad smiling and nodding as I share my thoughts and reactions about the letter. I can tell he's as excited as I am.

After a bit, though, I pause. "I have to admit, Dad—the roller coaster concept really spoke to me. One day, I feel happy and good about myself, and everything I do turns out right. But the next day, everything I do seems to turn out wrong. I feel unhappy, I lose heart, and I feel discouraged. And that, in turn, affects how I perform."

"Son, I know what you mean," he says, his voice comforting and calm. "I too occasionally struggle with the roller coaster effects. We need to learn the steps that put us in the best possible position to remain confident and secure during the roller coaster ride. That's why the next life skill letter is about how to be a peak performer in the midst of life's ups and downs. Peak performers can maintain a good self-image even when they're temporarily knocked off their feet."

"Peak performer," I repeat. "I like the sound of that."

"Good, because the next letter is coming your way soon! In the meantime, I want you to do some more homework."

"Got it," I say as I quickly scramble to find a pen and paper.

"I want you to think about three questions. First, what factors affect your self-image? Second, when your self-image takes a hit, how do you attempt to restore it? Third, when life knocks you down, what steps do you take to get back up on your feet as quickly as possible?"

I scribble as fast as I can.

"Look for the next letter tomorrow morning. Think you're ready?"

Without hesitating, I say, "I'm in. Let's go!"

CHAPTER TWO

ENSURING PEAK PERFORMANCE

The next morning, my phone beeps before my alarm again. For a moment, I'm confused about who would be emailing this early. Then I remember my agreement with Dad, and I fly out of bed.

I decide to once again use my shower time to consider the questions for today's lesson. I think about the things affecting my self-image: my own negative self-talk, demeaning comments from others, comparing myself to others, and dwelling on past setbacks. Whenever life knocks me down, I tend to lose hope easily, and it takes me a long time to get back on my feet.

Admittedly, I'm experiencing that now. Not having a job is a hit to my self-image. I'm not feeling like much of a peak performer.

After my shower, I get my cup of coffee, go into my office, quietly close the door, and sit down at my desk. I'm ready to read Dad's next letter. I'm really curious about this topic of peak performance, because I haven't been able to hold onto my confidence when life throws me curveballs.

I wonder how this will work.

Dear Son,

Today we will focus on how to remain confident and secure to ensure peak performance through the ups and downs of life. Peak performers know how to do their very best, no matter what life tosses at them. It's easy to think these people have some sort of "secret" or "superpower." But really, each and every one of us can be a peak performer once we learn how to see ourselves and our lives through God's eyes—not the world's.

FACTORS OF PERFORMANCE

Experts in psychology tell us that six factors determine how well we will perform: thoughts, self-image, beliefs, expectations, attitude, and feelings. Each factor builds upon the next, in a sequence.

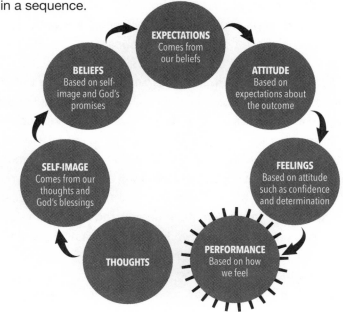

You can see how our thoughts are critical. They start the progression. Our thoughts shape our self-image, or how we see ourselves. And more importantly, how God sees us. In turn, our self-image creates the belief in whether we can or cannot accomplish something. This then creates an expectation whether we will or will not accomplish it—which is our expected outcome.

We then turn this expectation of the outcome into our attitude. A positive attitude can, in turn, create feelings of confidence and determination; a negative attitude creates feelings of hopelessness and inadequacy. And those feelings are what define our performance.

If you'd like a simpler version of the sequence, a Christian psychologist friend of mine reduced these six factors of performance down to just two: thoughts and feelings. He determined that our *thoughts* define how we *feel*, and how we *feel* defines how we *perform*.

Over the years, many people have asked me whether addressing these six factors from Psychology 101 can actually lead to peak performance. My short answer is yes. However, the answer is yes *only* if you base it all on who you are in God's eyes, not the world's.

As we've discussed, thoughts are the first factor in the sequence toward performance. If you focus your thoughts on who you are in God's eyes, you will create a positive, secure self-image. In turn, a secure self-image will create the belief that, yes, you can accomplish great things. This will then create the expectation that, yes, you will accomplish it—you will have faith in the outcome. You will then fuel this positive expectation into a confident, determined attitude. In turn, that attitude will create positive feelings. It's easy to see how this all leads to peak performance.

Again, the key here is who you are in God's eyes. If you base your thoughts on who you are in the world's eyes, you are in for a rough ride. Every day, we hear and read worldly messages that can make us feel insignificant and insecure. These negative messages can fill us with thoughts such as "I feel unworthy" and "I don't think I can . . ." It's difficult to perform well when such negative thoughts hold us back.

Also, the world's beliefs and standards change quickly. This is why we feel the roller coaster effect with the ups and downs.

When one of my Christian friends started working, he told me how his self-image and confidence went to extremes. He'd either feel high as a kite or so low that he could walk under a closed door. When he made a sale, he felt upbeat. But if a potential customer was unreceptive to his sales pitch, he felt discouraged and at times even depressed. He told me those feelings would last for days.

At one time in my life, I could identify with that friend. But fortunately, my mentor Martin taught me that when I feel insignificant, discouraged, or defeated, I need to replace my negative thoughts with the truth and knowledge of who I am in God's eyes. Unlike the world's standards, God's blessings and promises never change, because God never changes (Hebrews 13:8).

GOD'S BLESSINGS AND PROMISES

Everyone knows that we perform better when we feel significant and secure. If you find it difficult to feel significant and secure, the best solution is to turn to God's Word.

While reading and studying the Bible in 1982, I found fourteen verses I wish to share with you now. Six verses teach us about God's blessings, which provide significance to our lives. In addition, eight verses teach us about God's promises, which provide security for every believer. In order to make these verses more meaningful, I personalized them, and you should too.

God's Blessings Provide Our Significance

- I am His child (John 1:12).
- I am Christ's friend (John 15:15).
- I am a joint heir with Christ (Romans 8:17)
- God loves me (John 3:16; Jeremiah 31:3).
- I am precious in His sight (Isaiah 43:4).
- I am valuable (Matthew 6:26).

God's Promises Provide Our Security

- God forgives my sins (1 John 1:9).
- I am free from condemnation (Romans 8:1).
- God is always with me (Matthew 28:20).
- Nothing can separate me from God's love (Romans 8:35).
- God is for me. Who can be against me? (Romans 8:31)
- In all things, God works for my good (Romans 8:28).
- God's plan is for my welfare and to give me a future and a hope (Jeremiah 29:11).
- I can do all things in Him who strengthens me (Philippians 4:13).

Put a copy of these fourteen verses on your smartphone. Whenever you feel insignificant or insecure, read them for comfort and guidance. It's an easy way to use both Psychology 101 and God's Word in the "real world" so you can strive for peak performance.

God's promises provide our security and help us renew our mind (Romans 12:2) in times of trouble, so we can live a full and abundant life (2 Peter 1:4). The fact is, we will continually face problems in this world. Note that Jesus did not say that we *may* face problems. Instead, He said that we *will* face them (John 16:33).

Whenever you're facing an issue, or whenever you feel your performance falling short, look to the promises for a solution. For example, perhaps your performance falls short because you engaged in negative self-talk. Replace that negative thought with one of God's promises such as "I can do all things in him who strengthens me." Or if your performance falls short because your self-image took a hit, focus on one of God's blessings such as "I am precious in His sight."

I read these fourteen verses whenever life knocks me down. Does that mean I immediately get back on my feet? No. But when I keep focusing my thoughts on God's blessings (His assurances of my significance) and His promises (His assurances of my security), I find myself back on my feet before too long.

Here's a personal example of being knocked down and getting back up—over and over. One time, I was trying to convince a prospective client to do business with me instead of with my competitor. Even though I spent hours preparing what I thought was a compelling case, the client decided to hire my competitor. Their decision knocked me to the ground.

But then, three new clients hired me. I was feeling great again . . . until more problems arose. For the next four days, I experienced one rejection after another. What a roller coaster—up, down, up, down.

Instead of feeling discouraged, I reread and refocused on God's promises. First, I believed that even though I did not make the sale, God was still working for my good (Romans 8:28). Second, I believed that God had a plan for my welfare and my future (Jeremiah 29:11). Third, I believed that if I trusted in God's strength, I could do all things (Philippians 4:13). As a result, I was able to get on my feet quickly and continue to perform well.

If you want to be a peak performer, you need to read, reread, and focus on God's blessings and promises until they become a habit of thought. God's Word is truth (John 17:17), and His truth will set you free (John 8:32). Specifically, God's blessings and promises will set you free from doubt, discouragement, and fear. Focusing on, relying on, and acting on God's Word puts me—and will also put you—in the best position to continue being a peak performer.

HOPE AND PEAK PERFORMANCE

Life has its ups and downs, but sometimes life becomes so difficult that you lose hope. You may turn to the promise of "In all things, God works for my good," only to find yourself still struggling. Sometimes it's quite difficult to believe that the circumstance that knocked you down could *ever* work for your good.

I understand how you could feel that way. But it is critical that you do not lose hope from extreme difficulties. Hopelessness can severely impact your performance.

In times like this, you should study the life of the apostle Paul. If anyone should have lost hope, it was him. He was repeatedly knocked down.

So what did he say and do in response? Paul told us he was afflicted in every way, but not crushed. He was perplexed, but he didn't give up. He got knocked down, but he got back up again and kept going (2 Corinthians 4:8–10).

So how was Paul able to maintain hope and get back up on his feet quickly? The answer is found in 2 Corinthians 4:14–18. I recommend you read these verses tonight. Even though his outer nature was wasting away, he knew that his inner nature was being renewed every day. Also, Paul did not focus on what he saw and what he was experiencing. Instead, he focused on eternal things, such as God and the Holy Spirit.

Paul knew that the same Holy Spirit who raised Jesus from the dead would raise him—and would raise us. Specifically, Paul said, "If the Spirit of him who raised Jesus from the dead dwells in you, he who raised Christ Jesus from the dead will give life to your mortal bodies also through his Spirit which dwells in you" (Romans 8:11, RSV).

As believers, we know that the Holy Spirit lives in us. Like Paul, we need to rely on the enabling power of the Holy Spirit to help us maintain hope, to help us get up off the ground, and to help us continue being peak performers. The Holy Spirit gives you the power to perform well. Even though someone can show you what to do and how to do it, only the Holy Spirit can provide the power needed to apply what you learned (Zechariah 4:6; Acts 1:8; Ephesians 3:20; Romans 8:11).

In addition to focusing on the Holy Spirit, we must focus on Jesus and not on our problems. As I mentioned before, Peter could walk on water when he focused on Jesus and not on the waves and wind. But when Peter took his eyes off Jesus and focused on the wind and waves—his problems—he lost hope and began to sink.

Therefore, even if your present troubles make it difficult to identify with some of God's promises and blessings, you can still have hope by keeping your eyes on Jesus. At the same time, remember that the Holy Spirit, who raised Jesus from the dead, lives inside you and provides all the power you need to be a peak performer.

One time, a businessman asked me whether the same reasoning about hope would help someone who lost a spouse, a parent, a child, or a close friend to an unexpected death, a terminal illness, or a fatal accident. I told him it would, though that individual would still experience pain and sorrow for a period of time. I understand this firsthand.

Until fourteen years ago, I thought that I had everything figured out. Sure, I had my ups and downs, but God always seemed to work my downs for my good, just as the promise from Romans 8:28 states.

But then my best male friend (your mother is my best friend overall) was killed in a motorcycle accident. He left a wife and three children. It was brutal.

Initially, I was upset and angry with God. I doubted how my friend's death could work for the "good" of his wife and children or for the "good" of his parents and the friends who loved him.

Soon, I realized an important point: my friend had been a believer, and he was in heaven. And knowing that provided me hope.

I admit that I have no definitive answer for tragedies like this. We don't always understand God's ways. But God's Word helps by revealing how we can maintain hope (Deuteronomy 29:29).

God's Word commands us to love and trust Him. And if we do that, He will provide His love and give us hope. It also shows us the way to eternal life. In fact, God's own Son died a sudden, terrible death so that our sins could be forgiven and so we could obtain eternal life.

Therefore, even though we may continue to carry a sense of sorrow and loss with a tragic death, we believers know we will be reunited in heaven with our believing loved ones. We will live with them in heaven not for just a short time, as we did on earth, but for all eternity. God Himself will be with us, and there will be no more pain, sorrow, or tears (Revelation 21:3–4).

My business friend and I discussed another verse that says, "For those who live according to the flesh set their minds on the things of the flesh, but those who live accord-ing to the Spirit set their minds on the things of the Spirit. To set the mind on the flesh is death, but to set the mind on the Spirit is life and peace" (Romans 8:5–6, RSV).

Those verses tell us that every person on earth is in one of two groups. The favorite word for the first group is *I*. They view the events and trials of life through their own eyes. They try to control their life without God's help. No wonder they often feel hopeless.

The favorite word for the second group is *God*. They view the events and trials of life through God's eyes, and they allow the Holy Spirit to control their life. As a result, the Holy Spirit gives them love and peace (Galatians 5:22). Being in this latter group does not insulate you from tragedies. However, it does give you hope.

I concluded my conversation with my business friend by telling him that if my dear deceased friend could talk to us from heaven, he would tell us to make sure that everyone becomes a believer. And to someone who was not a believer, he would tell them the importance of making that decision today—because they could be dead in a second. That is why God's Word says, " . . . Behold, now is the acceptable time; behold, now is the day of salvation" (2 Corinthians 6:2, RSV).

THE ONE THING

Now that I have concluded my comments on how to ensure peak performance, you should identify and act on one thing you learned. As I mentioned in my last letter, after you make that one thing a habit, you can identity and act on another. Take one step at a time.

For example, because you know how thoughts begin the sequence toward performance, you may want to focus on replacing negative thoughts with God's blessings and promises. Ask God to help you do that, and ask the Holy Spirit to provide the power.

I want you to know how very proud I am of you for taking these steps. You will be amazed when you look back.

Love,

Dad

I am feeling a little overwhelmed again, but I also feel kind of excited about having tools to help me be a peak performer at all times. I really appreciate his suggestion of replacing my negative thoughts with God's blessings and promises. And it makes sense that our thoughts determine how we feel, and that how we feel determines how we perform.

I can start that right away. I can refer to God's blessings and promises each morning and when I am feeling low.

I want to tell Dad how I am going to follow his suggestions from this letter. I also want to see what my homework for the next topic will be.

So I call him. I make sure I have a pen and paper handy this time.

When Dad answers, I thank him for his insights as well as his practical instructions about peak performance. I tell him I will focus on how to apply God's blessings, promises, and resources.

Then I say, "You're going to discuss attitude in tomorrow's letter, aren't you? Even though I understand the importance of maintaining a positive attitude, I must admit I struggle with it. So, what are my homework questions?"

Dad laughs. "It's great to see you so excited for the next letter! Yes, it is about attitude. Your homework questions about attitude are simple: First, what factors affect your attitude? Second, what action steps can you take each day to maintain a positive attitude?"

"OK, great! I'll be all set before I read the letter. Thanks very much, Dad!"

"It is truly my pleasure, son."

CHAPTER THREE
MAINTAINING A POSITIVE ATTITUDE

As I sit sipping my coffee, I begin to think about my homework questions on attitude. I'm a little stumped.

I look out the window as I ponder. The days are getting lighter earlier. That's nice.

I turn my mind back to the task at hand. I know one thing for sure: I tend to focus on the negative rather than the positive. And I also let people around me pull me down. If they are in a bad mood, I end up in a bad mood, too.

I sometimes try to force myself to have positive feelings, but that seldom works. I usually revert to my old negative focus. It's hard to maintain those positive feelings for very long, let alone all day, every day.

It all feels heavy on my shoulders. With a deep breath, I open Dad's letter. I'm confident he'll have good answers to these questions. I'm excited to see what he has to say.

Good Morning, Son,

As I mentioned in yesterday's letter about peak performance, attitude is based on our expectations about outcomes. In turn, our expectations about outcomes are based on our beliefs. Our beliefs are based on our self-image. And our self-image comes from our thoughts. For our purposes in this letter, though, let's simply say that our attitude comes from our thoughts.

The good news is that we can choose what we think. For example, each morning when we wake up, we can choose to think positive thoughts that will give us a good attitude, or we can choose to think negative thoughts that will give us a poor attitude.

One problem we face, however, is that even when we start the day with a good attitude, our attitude can be affected by circumstances.

But even if something bad happens, you can choose your attitude—how you think about it. You can also choose whether to let another person's attitude affect yours.

So let's get started by defining the word *attitude*.

ATTITUDE DEFINED

Dictionaries provide several definitions of attitude. One definition is that attitude is a habit of thought. But my favorite definition states that attitude is simply the way you look at things.

For example, do you see a glass half full, or do you see a glass half empty? Many experts use that example to show the difference between an optimistic attitude and a pessimistic attitude.

Your mom is the perfect example of an eternal optimist. She always views life as a glass half full. In fact, Mom is so optimistic, I'm confident she could make a good argument that the glass half full is actually full!

Our attitude has four components: mental, spiritual, emotional, and physical. That is, we experience and express attitude in our minds, souls, hearts, and bodies. Later in the letter, I'll discuss how you can focus on these four areas to help maintain a positive attitude.

FACTORS THAT CAN AFFECT YOUR ATTITUDE

Both internal and external factors can affect your attitude. Internal factors include such things as focusing on positive or negative thoughts and engaging in positive or negative self-talk.

What thoughts do you focus on? Is your self-talk positive or negative?

It's hard to keep ourselves from slipping into negative thoughts or self-talk. The good news is, though, that nothing prevents you from replacing those negative ideas with positive ones. Here are some examples of how you can change your self-talk:

- "This is impossible" ➡ "All things are possible"
- "I doubt" ➡ "I believe"
- "I can't" ➡ "I can"

While you were growing up, you often said, "I can't do it." I'm sure you remember the day I handed you a small dictionary and asked you to look up the word *can't* and read the definition out loud.

You looked for the word, but couldn't find it. "*Can't* isn't in the dictionary," you said.

"You're right," I said. "There's no such word as *can't*."

What you didn't realize was that this was a special dictionary I used with you kids. I had used a razor blade to cut out the word *can't*.

Besides the internal factors, external factors can also affect your attitude. These include negative experiences you encounter at home, school, and work. On occasion, I even found that experiences *on the way to* work affected my attitude, especially when someone suddenly cut in front of me. Let's just say that the person who cut me off did not create an attitude of gratitude.

However, I believe that the most important factor that affects our attitude is our beliefs. As we learned in yesterday's letter, our beliefs ideally should come from God's Word in the form of His blessings and promises, such as, "I am a child of God," "I can do all things in him who strengthens me," and "In everything God works for my good."

WHY IS IT IMPORTANT TO
MAINTAIN A POSITIVE ATTITUDE?

Thomas Jefferson once said, "Nothing can stop the man with the right mental attitude from achieving his goal; nothing on earth can help a man with the wrong mental attitude." The quote doesn't say that knowledge, timing, resources, or money are what help someone achieve a goal. Rather, it implies that the right attitude is the most important element.

I agree—attitude is critical. Not only is attitude imperative in achieving goals but experts agree that people with positive attitudes are healthier and happier than people with negative attitudes.

We must also remember that our attitude—whether positive or negative—has ripple effects on our family, friends, and coworkers. Just ask yourself whether you enjoy being around people who are positive or negative. You know the answer.

When we're faced with a problem at home or work, it's not uncommon to adopt a negative attitude. We then direct this negativity toward the problem, the enemy.

But here's the important point: your enemy is not your spouse, coworker, boss, or any other human. On the contrary, your enemy is the devil, who wants you to have a negative outlook on life. As you'll see in the next section, remembering that the devil is our adversary is a key piece in maintaining a positive attitude.

The bad news is, our enemy is working against us in every way possible. The good news is, you can ask for God's help to resist the devil. And if you do, he will flee (James 4:7).

Jesus tells us that in this world we will have tribulations. But He also tells us to be of good cheer because He has overcome the world (John 16:33). Therefore, it is important to focus your trust and hope in Jesus.

Romans 15:13 (RSV) sums it up: "May the God of hope fill you with all joy and peace in believing, so that by the power of the Holy Spirit you may abound in hope."

WHAT ACTION CAN YOU TAKE TO MAINTAIN A POSITIVE ATTITUDE?

If you want to maintain a positive attitude, here are five steps you can take to begin each day. Starting the day on the right foot is key.

Step 1: Start Each Day in God's Word

Earlier, I mentioned that there are four components to attitude: mental, spiritual, emotional, and physical. So let's focus on this first step from each angle.

- **Mental Component**: Remember that the battle for our attitude starts in our mind. The devil wants to control it. The devil lies; there is no truth in him (John 8:44). He disguises himself as an angel of light (2 Corinthians 11:14).

  Remember too that we can choose what we think. So choose thoughts based on God's Word.

- **Spiritual Component:** Once again, we need to be aware that our battle is not against flesh and blood but against the devil. We need to fight this battle with spiritual weapons—even when it comes to our attitude.

  At the beginning of every day, pray that God will give you the spiritual weapons found in Ephesians 6:13–17. These include truth, the breastplate of righteousness, the gospel of peace, the shield of faith that stops the devil's flaming darts, the helmet of salvation, and the sword of the Spirit, which is God's Word.

  You may recall when your mom gave each of the grandchildren six boxes, one for each piece of spiritual armor. As the kids opened each box, Mom explained what the particular armor was and what it was used for. The kids had a great time with that and were full of questions. Your mother beamed!

- **Emotional Component:** Emotions can get out of hand if we let them. It's easy to see how this could lead to a negative attitude.

  Each morning, we need to ask the Holy Spirit to control our emotions and guide us to live by faith. God knows that our emotions can deceive us. Therefore, He wants us to walk by faith and not by sight (2 Corinthians 5:7).

- **Physical Component:** I think we all know that if we don't feel well, it's difficult to have a positive attitude. Therefore, we must take care of ourselves. We need to exercise, get adequate sleep and rest, and eat good, nutritious food.

Step 2: Keep an Attitude of Gratitude

God's Word tells us to always be joyful (1 Thessalonians 5:16) and to give thanks in everything (1 Thessalonians 5:18). Therefore, start each day with an attitude of gratitude.

Thank God, for He is good (Psalm 106:1). Don't take your life for granted. Thank God for giving you another day of life. You may find it helpful to tape the following verse to your bathroom mirror: "This is the day which the LORD has made; let us rejoice and be glad in it" (Psalm 118:24, RSV).

You may even decide to write a note or poem to remind you to stay positive with a thankful, can-do attitude. For example, when I first became a believer, I wrote the following poem and taped it to my bathroom mirror:

> *I wake up in the morning*
> *at 6:45.*
> *Good morning, God;*
> *I'm happy and alive.*
> *Your energy starts a flowing*
> *through my body and soul.*
> *I feel so good;*
> *I'm raring to go.*
> *Given any task,*
> *I'm more than capable.*
> *I'm focused and optimistic;*
> *I'm unstoppable.*

Step 3: Keep the Same Attitude as Jesus

God's Word tells us to have the same attitude as Jesus (Philippians 2:5). We know that if God asks us to do something, He provides the enabling power through the Holy Spirit. Therefore, ask God to help you maintain a positive attitude throughout the day, and ask the Holy Spirit to provide the power.

Step 4: Fill Your Mind with God's Word

Society is becoming more negative. Every day, people and media bombard us with negative words, statements, ideas, and images that can erode our self-image and create discouragement and despair.

Just as we discussed in the first letter, we need to counteract this flow of garbage with God's Word. Therefore, ask God to fill your mind with thoughts that are true, honorable, just, pure, lovely, gracious, excellent, and worthy of praise (Philippians 4:8).

Step 5: Fill Your Mind with God's Blessings and God's Promises

Calling back to the second letter, ask God to fill your mind with His blessings, which provide our significance, and His promises, which provide our security. I personalized these in the letter from yesterday. You've already started referring to these blessings and promises in the morning to replace your negative thoughts with positive thoughts.

ATTITUDE CHECK

Even though taking these five action steps will help you maintain a positive attitude throughout the day, there will be times when you need an attitude check. For instance, maybe some unexpected external event changes your attitude.

For whatever reason you may need an attitude check, here are a few questions to ask yourself, followed by a corresponding corrective action:

Question: Is my "stinkin' thinkin'" the result of negative self-talk? Am I saying, "I can't do this"?

Action: If so, I should replace "I can't" with "I can."

Question: Is my poor attitude the result of my self-image taking a hit?

Action: If so, I should reread the list of God's blessings that provide significance.

Question: Is my poor attitude the result of focusing on my problems?

Action: If so, I should reread the list of God's promises, which provide my security and the right focus.

Question: Is my poor attitude the result of out-of-control emotions?

Action: If so, I should ask God to help me live by faith (Galatians 2:20).

Question: Is my poor attitude the result of feeling unsupported?

Action: If so, I should ask God to surround me with people who support me.

THE ONE THING

When it comes to maintaining a positive attitude, what is one thing you can do today?

Maybe for you, it's to start each morning with an attitude of gratitude and to ask God to give you the power to keep that attitude throughout the day.

I know you can do it.

Love,

Dad

I can't believe it—I'm really excited this time! This letter was so helpful.

For years, I've thought that my attitude depended on the people around me. I've been trying to make sure the "right" people were around me all the time, just so I could maybe keep a positive attitude.

But I had my eye on the wrong ball! I don't need to follow people. I need to follow God. And by following Him and believing in His promises and blessings, I can put myself in a position to maintain the right attitude all day long.

I grab the phone and call Dad.

When he answers, he chuckles before he even says hello. "Well, it seems you're reading faster every morning! What did you think about this one?"

"Dad, I loved it! This is great! If I feel myself slipping into a negative attitude, I can do an attitude check and get rid of the stinkin' thinkin'!"

This gets a loud guffaw from Dad! It's great to hear him laugh. It makes me smile too.

"Well, son, I couldn't be more pleased. But we're just getting warmed up. Tomorrow I'll be talking about creating and maintaining balance. We must balance many facets in life: spiritual, family, career, mental, emotional, physical, financial, and social needs. So, tonight I want you to think about three things: One, what does a balanced life mean to you? Two, list one thing you would like to address in each of the eight life-balance facets. Three, draw a model of what a balanced life looks like to you."

As always, I scribble quickly to keep up. "Wow, it sounds like this will be another great letter."

"I'm looking forward to seeing what you think of this one. Have a productive afternoon. I love you!"

"I love you too, Dad! Thanks—and I'll talk to you tomorrow!"

CHAPTER FOUR

CREATING AND MAINTAINING BALANCE

It's morning again–time to read Dad's next letter. I feel like I need to spend a little extra time thinking about my homework today. I was feeling pretty enthusiastic yesterday, but now as I'm reading my notes, I'm not sure how to answer his questions about balancing all eight facets in life: spiritual, family, career, mental, emotional, physical, financial, and social needs.

What does a balanced life mean to me? What is one thing I'd like to address in each of the eight facets? How can I draw a model of what a balanced life looks like to me? Eight facets seem like a lot. How can I do this?

It seems impossible, but I'll give it a shot. I know Dad will show me how through his advice in the letter, but I just can't see it right now.

OK, I know I want eternal life—that goes with the spiritual facet.

As far as family goes, of course I want a loving relationship with my wife and children.

In the career facet, I just want a job, any job, right now.

The mental facet . . . ? I feel like it takes me too long to figure things out sometimes. Maybe I just want to be able to process information faster and more clearly.

Emotionally, I want to be happy. That one is simple.

I also want to maintain a healthy weight and feel good, so that would be under the physical facet.

Before I turn seventy, I want to have enough money to live independently, so that would go with financial.

Socially? It would be amazing to have at least one friend who loves me unconditionally.

That's all eight, I guess. I'm not going to make this diagram too complicated, though. I'll just make a pie chart with eight equal parts. I think that's what Dad meant for me to do, anyway. As for what to put in the center . . . I have no idea!

With that, I hold my breath and start reading the letter.

My Dear Son,

This letter will focus on how to create and maintain a balanced life. According to most dictionaries, balance is a state of bodily equilibrium, including mental and emotional stability. I consider that state of balance to include the eight facets I mentioned when we talked yesterday: spiritual, family, career, mental, emotional, physical, financial, and social needs.

A businessman I once mentored told me his definition of a balanced life. To him, having a balanced life means having a handle on all eight areas of his life, so that his mind and heart do not feel as if they are being pulled too hard in any one direction.

Initially, I too thought I had to maintain equal balance in all eight areas. The Ecclesiastes 3:1–8 verses informed me, however, that there's a time for everything. For example, there's a time to work hard, and there's a time to play hard.

BALANCE

Eventually, I discovered that balance does not mean equal parts. The life we live on earth has a certain ebb and flow. I realized it's often necessary to place a different emphasis on one or more of the eight areas, depending on current life circumstances.

For example, when I started my CEO job, I had to work extra hours. But after several months of working late, your mother told me I needed to spend more time with our family. Therefore, I had to make a change to balance my commitment to work and my responsibility to my family. In short, work had become too dominant. I lost balance, and it caused conflict and unhappiness at home.

To regain my lost balance, I needed to reorganize my lifestyle. In addition to cutting back on the time I spent working late at the office, I also cut back on the time I spent on my weekend hobbies and interests so that I could spend more time with our family.

So, where are you out of balance? What is important to you? And what are you going to rebalance?

Remember that your model can change depending on your stage in life and your current circumstances. In other words, it's not enough to create a model for a balanced life that works for you now; you must also be ready to adjust it from time to time.

The Center of Your Model

Let me share a conversation I had with a businessman during a flight to Chicago years ago—before I knew how to live my best life through God's Word. He and I shared our respective vocations and avocations, and we got to talking about life balance.

He told me that we all have a choice on how we decide to balance our lives. We can either live according to the world's view or according to God's view.

Then he pulled out a piece of paper and started writing and drawing. He created a life-balance model depicting those who live according to the world's view.

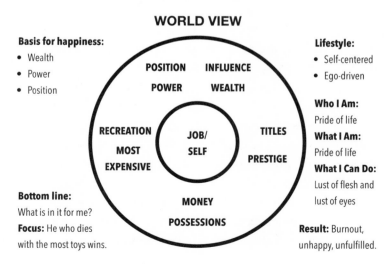

WORLD VIEW

Basis for happiness:
- Wealth
- Power
- Position

POSITION   INFLUENCE
POWER   WEALTH

RECREATION   JOB/   TITLES
MOST   SELF
EXPENSIVE   PRESTIGE

MONEY
POSSESSIONS

Lifestyle:
- Self-centered
- Ego-driven

Who I Am:
Pride of life
What I Am:
Pride of life
What I Can Do:
Lust of flesh and
lust of eyes

Bottom line:
What is in it for me?
Focus: He who dies
with the most toys wins.

Result: Burnout,
unhappy, unfulfilled.

As I studied the model, I realized he was describing the way I lived.

He told me that the world's basis for happiness is wealth, power, and position. Yes, that was me. He said that this life-style is self-centered and ego driven. Yes, that was me.

He said the center of the circle was job and self. Right again—my identity was my job, and my life was about me. This was something my mentor Martin had already discussed with me, actually. He told me that whatever is at the center of your life is where you get your self-image, security, and power. He told me that the problem with putting your job at the center of your life is that jobs change and will eventually come to an end. Then what happens to your self-image, security, and power? They could tank, and so could you.

Right above the center circle, the businessman wrote *position*, *power*, *influence*, and *wealth*. How true. They were my focus.

Working around the circle in a clockwise direction were the words *titles* and *prestige*. Yes, title and prestige were my goals. Next came *money* and *possessions*. Yes, indeed. Money and possessions were most important to me.

Then came *recreation*. Of course, only the most expensive forms of recreation would satisfy those who live under the world's view. Like many, my mantra was "He who dies with the most toys wins."

For those who choose to live according to the world, the bottom line is the question, "What's in it for me?" Oh yes. This was a question I asked myself on a daily basis.

But then came the downside, the businessman explained: many who live by this view end up unhappy, unfulfilled, and burned out. Using the world's view as a measure for balance subjects us to a changeable standard and unquenchable need—need for more wealth, prestige, recognition, and power. But it is never enough.

How depressing, I thought. Then I realized, *What if I spend the next thirty to forty years climbing the corporate ladder and living according to the world's view, only to discover that I've climbed the wrong ladder with no time for a "do-over"? That would be brutal!*

Needless to say, the man had my attention. Now he was going to draw the life-balance model for living by God's view. I was extremely interested to see his model and to hear what he had to say about it.

He told me that for those who choose to live under God's view, the basis for happiness is their relationship with God, daily spiritual food, and loving and serving others. When he showed me his God's-view model, the first thing I noticed was the Holy Trinity—God the Father, God the Son, and God the Holy Spirit—right at the center. The Holy Trinity is eternal, and the three members never change. They are all-wise and all-powerful, and they remain the same yesterday, today, tomorrow, and forever.

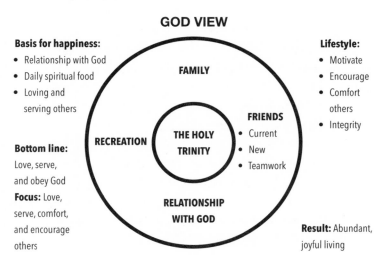

GOD VIEW

Basis for happiness:
- Relationship with God
- Daily spiritual food
- Loving and serving others

Bottom line:
Love, serve, and obey God
Focus: Love, serve, comfort, and encourage others

FAMILY

THE HOLY TRINITY

RECREATION

FRIENDS
- Current
- New
- Teamwork

RELATIONSHIP WITH GOD

Lifestyle:
- Motivate
- Encourage
- Comfort others
- Integrity

Result: Abundant, joyful living

In a ring around the center were family, friends, recreation, and relationship with God. Instead of having a self-centered and ego-driven lifestyle, people who live under God's view want to motivate, encourage, and comfort others. Having friends is more important than titles and prestige. Having a relationship with God is more important than money and possessions. Yes, recreation is important, but it does not have to be the best and most expensive recreation. In fact, it's most likely recreation that also provides you quality time with friends and family.

The bottom line of living according to God's view is not "What's in it for me?" Instead, the bottom line is to love, serve, and obey God. The focus is not "He who dies with the most toys wins," but rather to love, serve, comfort, and encourage others.

Then comes the result of a life balance according to God's view. It's not burnout, unhappiness, and lack of fulfillment, but rather abundant, joyful living. In other words, a life of happiness that lasts. You already know this, son, because that was the theme of our first letter.

Life-Balance Action Plan

Once you choose to balance your life according to God's view, the next step is to figure out a plan to put that new balance into action. In order to help you know what needs balance in your life, take a seven-day time inventory to track how much time you spend on each of the eight areas of your life.

After reviewing your time inventory, in what area do you spend the most time? Where do you spend the least time? What area in your life do you find is most out of balance? What is suffering as a consequence?

Maybe your time inventory will show what my time inventory initially showed, which was little or no time in the spiritual area. This is one reason why some people cannot find happiness that lasts.

Some people do time inventories, only to see that they spend too much time at the office plus working at home. They realize they need to make adjustments to rebalance their time between work and family. Don't say: "I don't have time. I'm just too busy." The truth is, we always find time to do what we want to do.

Let me give you an example of balancing. Social balance can be divided between time alone and time spent with others. Personally, I have a need for regular solitude, but I do also enjoy spending time with family and friends. Your mother once told me that when I spend too much time alone, I become more self-centered. But your mother also told me that if I spent too much time with others, I could experience a false sense of who I am based on others' opinions.

Your mother is wise, and I listened to her. I learned to balance between spending time alone and spending time with family and friends to keep from becoming either too self-centered or too self-important.

If you are like me, you may decide you need to balance the spiritual area. When I was in my early thirties, my mentor Martin told me that the spiritual area consists of God's five purposes and calls, which we discussed in the first letter about happiness.

Go back and review the five purposes and five calls. Then look at your time inventory to see how much time you spend each day on one or more of them. If the answer is none, prepare a plan for how you will start spending the necessary time.

To illustrate an exemplary life of balance, consider the life led by Jesus. What does God's Word say are the crucial areas of His life? The answer is found in Luke 2:52. This verse says that Jesus grew in wisdom (mental), in stature (physical), in favor with God (spiritual), and with man (social). Therefore, if you want to lead a balanced life like Jesus, ask yourself the following four questions:

1. What is your plan to grow in wisdom?

2. What is your plan to grow stronger and healthier physically?

3. What is your plan to grow in God's favor?

4. What is your plan to be more sociable?

The key to preparing a life-balancing plan and acting on it is to keep it simple. For example, maybe you want to gain wisdom. Your action plan could be to read one proverb and one psalm every day. As you read the proverb and the psalm, ask yourself what the point is and how you can apply it to your life.

The One Thing
What is one thing you learned from this letter that would have the biggest impact on your ability to create and maintain balance?

Maybe you realize that if you are not healthy and in good shape, you won't have the physical energy to keep your life balanced. If so, maybe you will decide to commit to thirty minutes of exercise every day, combined with a healthy diet and a good night's sleep. This could be a great place to start. But remember that you will continue to build on the things that you learn and implement one by one into your life. This one thing will be a basis for the next one thing.

I think I've given you plenty to work on for today. I look forward to talking with you!

Love,
Dad

Whew! Dad is right. This is plenty to think about.

Right away, I can see that the life-balance model I drew is all wrong. Dad said it right in the letter: it's unrealistic to think all eight areas can be equally balanced. And yes, I should have God at the center of my life. But I bet my time inventory would show that I need to do all sorts of rebalancing.

I grab my pen and paper as I dial Dad's number.

"Hello, son!"

"Hi, Dad." I sigh a little bit.

"Feeling a little overwhelmed today?"

"Yeah. I keep thinking about eight things I need to balance. It feels like so much. But I'll try to just focus on one at a time."

"Don't be too hard on yourself, son. This is a lifelong journey you're on. Let's keep it simple. What's the one thing you want to focus on from my email today?" He pauses.

I think for a minute.

"Well, I think I'll follow your suggestion to take better care of myself physically. I'm feeling kind of worn down with this job search. It's hard to justify taking time away for myself."

"And what will you now do differently?" He's silent again, waiting.

I think about what I've been doing to "treat" myself, because things have been tough lately. "I'm not going to give in and pick up a pizza for dinner," I say. "Instead, I'm going to take a walk every evening after we eat. And I'll make sure I'm in bed by ten each night. I know I can do at least this much." I feel a little uncertain, because it doesn't seem like enough.

But Dad's reaction surprises me. "That's excellent! A great beginning! If you do this every day, you'll notice a difference. Don't worry—you'll build on this as you move forward."

"Really? OK, great! Thanks!" I can actually feel myself grinning. What a relief!

"Definitely. I'm glad you're taking steps one by one. Tomorrow I'm going to discuss the topic of setting and achieving goals. I want you to think about one goal that, if achieved, would have the greatest impact on your life. It's a good one, so give it some thought."

I write down my assignment. "Yes, I will! Thanks, Dad. Thanks for being so supportive!"

"I'm glad to be there for you. I love you."

"Love you too, Dad. Talk to you tomorrow!"

CHAPTER FIVE

SETTING AND ACHIEVING GOALS

My eyes open wide. Is that the alarm? Yes, yes it is. It's starting to get light, and I can see shapes in my bedroom. I look at my wife. She hasn't budged—that's good, she doesn't need to get up just yet.

Dad's letter. We're doing goals today. What is my one goal? I realize I'd actually like to have more than one! Hmmpf. OK, then, what's the top goal that will have the greatest impact on my life?

I slowly roll out of bed, go to the living room, and look out at the garden. I have to be honest with myself: I really don't want to set a goal. Not because I don't want to improve my life or don't know what I want. I guess you could say I *have* goals. It's just that when I *set* them, it seems as if I always fail. Maybe I'm not strong enough or lack the willpower.

Then again, I have a feeling Dad's letter will tell me that goals have nothing to do with things such as strength and will-power. Maybe I have this all wrong.

Why don't I just read the letter, then decide what my one goal should be?

"Good idea!" I whisper out loud.

Dear Son,

Today I'm going to focus on setting and achieving goals. So just what is a goal? Most dictionaries define a goal as the ongoing pursuit of a worthy objective until accomplished.

Why should we have goals? Goals trigger the power of focus that enables us to accomplish more in a shorter period of time. Also, goals or targets coupled with an action plan provide a road map to help us move from where we are now to where we want to be.

When I was twelve years old, your grandfather told me that a person can't hit a target if they don't have one to aim at. To illustrate his point, he drove me to an old sandpit to do some target practice with his .22-caliber rifle. He set a paper target on the sandpit and walked back to where I was standing. He told me to aim at the bull's-eye and see how many times I could hit it. I aimed and fired. I was able to place several rounds in and around the bull's-eye.

Then your grandfather told me to put the gun down, and he walked out to retrieve the target. He came back and congratulated me on hitting the target. Next, he told me to reload the rifle and shoot in the direction of the sandpit. I asked him what I was supposed to shoot at. He was still holding the target.

"Good," he said. "That's the question to ask. You can't hit a target or a goal that you don't have to aim at. I know several smart, hard-working people who don't seem to accomplish much. The reason is they have not identified a clear target or goal to aim at."

ACTION PLAN TO ACHIEVE YOUR GOAL

Setting goals is important, but it's not enough in and of itself. Many people set goals, only to fall short. Why? Because they don't realize they also need an action plan to make it happen. Martin told me that a goal without an action plan is nothing but a wish. And as we all know, wishes don't magically come true on their own.

Now I want you to think a minute. Last year, did you set a goal? Did you reach it?

If the answer is yes, did you have an action plan? What steps did you take to reach it?

If you didn't reach it, spend a few minutes being honest with yourself about what happened. What went wrong? What would you do differently? What did you learn? Did you approach the goal with an action plan?

Let me share a success story of someone who achieved his goal. A friend of mine created a goal to lose twenty pounds in ten weeks. When I asked him how he achieved his goal, he said he took specific steps each day to reach it. He had an action plan.

You can use his action plan as a template to achieve your own goals. Let's explore each step now.

"Being" in the Right Mind-set

The first step to setting a goal is to have the right mind-set. This is something I myself have come to understand about setting goals. It technically wasn't part of my friend's action plan, though I'm certain he went through a similar thought process, even if he didn't label it.

Anyone who wants to achieve a goal needs to begin with the "be, do, have" mind-set. As we will soon discuss, the order of these words is specific, and it's what leads to success.

Many people, however, don't understand this order. Instead, they set goals from a "do, have, be" mind-set. They believe that if they *do* the right things, they'll *have* what they want, and they'll become the type of person they want to *be*.

Others try the "have, do, be" approach. They believe that if they can first *have* what they need, such as more money, they'll be able to *do* what they want, and then they'll become the type of person they want to *be*.

But again, the right order is "be, do, have." If you first focus on the type of person you want to *be*, you'll identify who you are and the values you want to live by. These values will guide your goal setting. You will fully know what you want to *do* or achieve. And only then you will understand what's truly important to *have* in life..

So, consider the kind of person you want to be, and ask yourself these questions: Do you want to be honest and trustworthy? Do you want to be a person of integrity? (I define integrity as continually doing the right thing, even when no one is watching.) Do you want to be responsible, dependable, and caring? Do you want to have an attitude of gratitude? Do you want to have a positive, persistent can-do attitude? Do you want to commit to excellence in everything you do? Do you want to be a likeable, respectful person?

If you answered yes to any of these questions, assess where you are now. If you haven't yet become the type of person you want to be, set a goal to move from who you are now to who you want to become. Learning to *be* the kind of person you want to be comes first. Then your goals, actions, and outcomes will be guided by your foundational values.

Aligning Goals and Motives with Values

The next step in your action plan is to intentionally set your goal. This step is more involved than you may think. It isn't as simple as just thinking up an idea. If you want to achieve your goal, you need to fully understand the motivation behind it and how it aligns with your values.

In setting your goals, you're motivated and guided by the principles and standards you want to live by. In short, you're motivated by your values. If you truly want to achieve the goal, your motivation needs to align with a value that is deeply important to *you*.

Notice the emphasis here. You should choose one goal that's important to *you*, one *you* want to achieve—not something someone else wants for you. If the goal isn't important to you at a value-based level, you'll never persevere.

How do you know if your goal aligns with your values? To begin, create a goal statement that's clear, specific, and measurable. Then ask yourself why it's important. Take your answer, then ask yourself why that too is important. And then take that next answer and ask yourself why that, in turn, is important. By the end, you'll have asked yourself three times why your goal is important to you. This will help you get to the real reason that aligns with your values. That will be the thing that motivates you.

Being honest with yourself as you ask the three *why* questions is vitally important because it allows you to identify your true motivation. Is your motive the right one for you? Is it founded on your values and who you are? Or is the goal what someone else wants for you?

For example, the first thing my friend did was to identify his goal of losing twenty pounds in ten weeks. Then he asked himself why that was important. He answered that he wanted to lose weight to reduce stress on his heart and knees, to lower his blood pressure, and to sleep better.

Then he asked the second why question: Why was it important to reduce stress on his heart and knees, lower his blood pressure, and sleep better? Because, he realized, he wanted to have more energy and put himself in the best possible position to live longer.

Next, he asked the third why question: Why was it important to have more energy and put himself in the best possible position to live longer? He realized he wanted to not be exhausted at the end of the day, so he could spend more quality time with his family—for many years to come.

This was the real reason he wanted to lose weight. By asking why three times, he narrowed his goal to something that aligned with his values.

With this in mind, he revised his goal statement to now include what he wanted to achieve as well as the true motivation behind it: "I will lose twenty pounds in ten weeks in order to have more energy, so I can enjoy time with my family and friends and so I can increase the likelihood that I will live longer." My friend's values clearly included quantity and quality time with his family, so that value gave him motivation to achieve his goal of losing weight.

Like my friend, start with a simple goal statement, then ask the three *why* questions. Once you discover how your goal aligns with your values, be sure to revise your goal statement to include your motivational "why." It will significantly increase the probability of achieving your goal.

Identifying and Overcoming Obstacles

After crafting his goal statement and motivation, my friend's next step was to honestly identify the obstacles that inevitably stood in his way. Obstacles are typically problems, and problems are normal. Remember in my third letter when we talked about maintaining a positive attitude? I cited that Jesus told us in John 16:33 that in this world, we *will* have problems, but that we should be of good cheer because He has overcome the world. That scripture applies here as well.

Because life is full of obstacles, it's important to anticipate what obstacles could keep you from your goal, and then figure out a plan to either avoid or overcome them. This part can be a little humbling, because you need to admit your weaknesses. That's because most obstacles are internal, not external. Yes, sometimes outside forces do get in our way of achieving our goals. But more often than not, we ourselves create our own obstacles.

Think of it this way: a goal is a plan for change. In order to change, however, you will need to overcome old habits, behaviors, and thoughts. Those old parts of your life could turn into obstacles holding you back.

That's why it's so important to identify these potential obstacles ahead of time. By anticipating and planning ahead, you won't be caught off guard. You'll know what to do, which will keep you from overreacting to your problem and making it worse.

In my friend's case, he identified several behaviors that could make it difficult to meet his goal of losing weight. First, he admitted that he often used the excuse of being "too busy" to exercise and keep track of what he ate. Second, he realized he enjoyed eating large portions of food, which would quickly thwart any weight-loss goals. Third, he knew he liked honey and other sweets too much to give them up.

So, before he even started his actual weight-loss plan, he prepared a detailed "pre-plan" on how to deal with obstacles and temptations before he was confronted by them.

To counter the "too busy" obstacle, he decided to exercise at least thirty minutes every day, no excuses. This would include lifting light weights and either walking outside or on a treadmill. He knew this would be much more effective than leaving exercise up to a "decision" each day.

To counter the problem of eating large portions, he decided to be more conscious about how much he ate at any meal. He realized he often ate without thinking, which quickly led to overeating. So before taking a single bite, he would determine how much he'd eat, then stop. This naturally led to smaller portions. For instance, instead of unwittingly eating five pieces of pizza, he would decide to eat only two.

When it came to sweets, he figured out that his emotions often trumped his rational thinking. Once again, he realized he often ate without thinking, especially when it came to sweets. He needed to be more intentional. His plan was to drink more water and unsweetened green tea instead of sugary drinks. He would also eat more salads (with dressing on the side) to help him feel full, which would cut down on the need for desserts. And for those times when he did want something sweet, he would replace ice cream and cookies with sugar-free gum and mints.

In particular, my friend knew that sugar would be a major obstacle—one he needed to learn more about. He did some research and found that too much sugar can create an overproduction of insulin that in turn creates more sugar cravings. He also discovered that sugar locks fat in the cells and prevents the fat from being used as a source of energy.

Armed with this new knowledge, my friend then looked at how much sugar he was consuming to start the day. He was shocked to learn it was over one hundred grams a day. For years, he had started each morning with what he thought was a healthy shake. He blended two cups of milk, one apple, one banana, a half cup of blueberries, one cup of kale, a half scoop of protein powder, and four tablespoons of honey. Suddenly he began to understand how his weight had shot up to 215 pounds.

Had he not done this extra research, he never would have realized how much of a problem those shakes could have posed to his weight-loss goal. He changed the contents of his shake, avoiding this problem altogether.

Putting the Action Plan in Motion

My friend put a considerable amount of thought and preparation into meeting his goal. He did more than jot down a generic goal statement. He took the time to make sure he knew what was motivating him, he was honest about where he would be tempted to go off track, and he planned how to avoid letting this happen.

With his action plan ready, my friend began his ten-week weight-loss program. It's important to note that every day he did something that moved him closer to reaching his goal. He read food labels, limited his sugar intake, exercised, and consumed fewer calories. Before taking any action during the day, he asked himself whether doing it would move him closer to or further from reaching and maintaining his goal.

I'm happy to say he met his goal and developed new healthy habits. Better yet, it gave him even more motivation to focus on the next goal that would have the greatest impact on his life.

Goals That Please God

Many of us have set weight-loss goals, like my friend's. Or maybe we've set goals to quit smoking, save more money, or do an important house project. These are good goals for everyday life, especially when we understand how they align with our values.

But sometimes we want to set goals that aren't so much about everyday life as they are about *eternal* life. Sometimes we want a goal that is not only deeply important to ourselves but also to God. It can be easy for our worldly goals to cloud our intentions to live a life to please God. To help you think of goals that would please God, here are some examples for you to consider:

To Leave a Legacy

What type of legacy do you want to leave? Your grandfather told me that one way to help ensure you will leave a positive legacy is to ask and answer this question: What do you want people to say at your funeral?

Think of your spouse, children, grandchildren, siblings, extended family, friends, employers, coworkers, and pastor or priest. After you write down what you would like each person to say about you, make it your goal to start living that way.

If you want to leave a positive legacy, don't do anything you wouldn't be proud to read in a newspaper or hear on the nightly news. Unfortunately, Bernie Madoff didn't follow this advice. Instead, he was responsible for a Ponzi scheme considered to be the largest financial fraud in US history. After the judge sentenced him, Madoff said, "I left a legacy of shame."

To Know the Three Eternals

As I mentioned in the first letter, these three are eternal: God, His Word, and People.

God's Word states that *God* is eternal (Deuteronomy 33:27; Isaiah 40:28; 1 Timothy 1:17). Assuming that you plan to spend eternity with *God*, you should get to know Him better. And how do you do that?

Through the second eternal, which is *God's Word* (Isaiah 40:8; Matthew 24:35; Mark 13:31; 1 Peter 1:25). How much time do you spend each day reading, studying, and applying God's Word to your life? Jesus told us, " . . . Man shall not live by bread alone, but by every word that proceeds from the mouth of God" (Matthew 4:4, RSV).

The third eternal is the *people* who will either spend eternity with God or be eternally separated from Him (1 John 5:11–13). How much time do you spend each day loving and serving people and sharing the gospel of God (1 Thessalonians 2:8)? Remember that God created us in Christ Jesus for good works (Ephesians 2:10).

As a refresher, you can reread God's Five Calls from my first letter for more on the three eternals.

To Become More Like Jesus

In order to become more like Jesus, we need to get to know Him. God's Word tells us that we already have the mind of Jesus (1 Corinthians 2:16). But do you use your mind to think as He thinks? Ask yourself these questions:

Do you love like Jesus? Do you love God with all your heart, soul, and mind (Matthew 22:37)? Do you love your neighbor as yourself (Matthew 22:39)?

Do you live like Jesus? Is your goal to serve and not to be served (Mark 10:45)? Are you a person of prayer who prays continually (1 Thessalonians 5:17)?

Do you labor like Jesus? Do you have compassion for people who are harassed and helpless (Matthew 9:36)?

To Witness for Jesus

Make it a goal to become a witness for Christ. God's Word tells us that we are the "aroma" of Christ (2 Corinthians 2:15).

If you want to become a witness, where do you start? A good place is to prepare your own testimony. This is essentially a statement or story about how you become a believer. No one can argue with you about your own personal testimony (2 Corinthians 5:17).

Before you prepare your personal testimony, you may want to read and incorporate the four steps Paul used for his testimony to King Agrippa (Acts 26:1–23): Paul establishes rapport and common ground (v. 2–3), tells King Agrippa about his life before he accepted Christ as his Lord and Savior (v. 4–12), tells how he came to know Jesus (v. 13–18), and then explains what his life was like after he came to know Jesus (v. 19–27).

Despite his testimony, Paul was unable to convince King Agrippa to accept Jesus as his Lord and Savior. But this unsuccessful attempt did not destroy Paul's confidence. Why? Because Paul knew that only God can save people. Paul was just a helper, and so are we. Therefore, when we share our personal testimony, we should feel no pressure.

Make it a goal, then, to share your personal testimony with others whenever the opportunity presents itself. It's a wonderful way to help transform lives by showing people how it looks and feels to be a believer. Remember, you don't need to feel pressured about obtaining a certain outcome from your sharing. Just let God's Word work in their heart.

To Fill a Spiritual Void

Before I accepted Christ, I thought that I was a happy, successful person. Nevertheless, I felt as if something was still missing. In short, I felt as if there was a void in my life.

As a result, I tried to fill the void with worldly things. But with the help of mentors, I came to realize my void was a spiritual void. And you can't fill a spiritual void with nonspiritual things.

My void remained until I began to read God's Word and involve Him in my daily life. This is when I found new peace. I became a kinder, more compassionate person. In fact, some company executives who worked for me commented that even though I still made tough decisions, I was more compassionate.

Might you have a spiritual void too? If so, how are you trying to fill it? Perhaps you need to set a goal to fill this spiritual void the right way: with God and His Word.

To Hear Jesus Say, "Well Done"

After you die, what are the first words you'd like to hear? How about making it one of your goals to hear Jesus say, " . . .

Well done, good and faithful servant . . . enter into the joy of your master" (Matthew 25:23, RSV).

God wants us to love and serve other people (1 Thessalonians 2:8). He wants us to do what is right, to love mercy, and to walk humbly with Him (Micah 6:8). Do you obey God's commandments? When you deal with people, do you do what is right?

God gives each of us at least one gift to help us love and serve others (1 Peter 4:10). For example, Romans 12:6–8 lists gifts and abilities from God that enable you to do certain things well and help others. To find your gift or gifts, consider the following list:

- **Prophecy:** Reading and interpreting Scripture
- **Service:** Giving practical help to those in need
- **Teaching:** Explaining the application of God's Word in the hearer's life
- **Encouragement:** Emboldening others
- **Contributing:** Doing a good job with your administrative abilities
- **Giving aid:** Sharing your time and money to help others
- **Leadership:** Using your leadership skills to serve God and others
- **Acts of mercy:** Showing acts of kindness to others

The One Thing

As you know, I end each letter by encouraging you to think of one thing you can take from this discussion and apply to your life. This time, how about thinking about one goal? If you remember, that was your homework before you started the letter, and now it's your homework after finishing it!

What is one goal—big or small—that would have great impact on your life? Perhaps it's to identify one gift God has given you to help others. Set a goal and action plan to use this gift—which you can then put to use in future goals that follow.

Love,

Dad

I smile and let out a little sigh. Just as I thought, Dad's letter explains the real secret behind achieving goals. Now I see that I don't approach goals very well. I never really get down to my values and motivation, and I never plan ahead about how to handle problems.

No wonder so many of my goals never work out. And here I thought I just needed to be "stronger." Now I know how to make a goal *and* an action plan.

But what about the one goal? I still don't really know what that might be.

I sit back in my chair and start thinking—only to hear my phone ring. It's Dad.

"Hello, son!" he greets.

"Hi, Dad! I just finished the letter," I say. "There's so much to think about!"

"Have you started thinking about the one thing—or the one goal, I should say?"

I cringe a little. If only I had had a few more minutes!

"Um . . . no, not really," I admit.

"Well," Dad says, "how about using the suggestion from the letter? Maybe your goal can be to identify and use a gift God has given you to help and encourage others."

Like that, something seems to open. "You know, that really is a great idea. I'm so preoccupied these days looking for a job and thinking about all my problems. I never think about how I can help others. I'd love to set a goal to use my gift of service." My thoughts and words come fast now. "I'll follow those action plan steps from your friend—starting by taking an honest look at my mind-set and whether I'm in the 'be, do, have' order. Man, this is great! I'm excited to start on it. I feel like I have the tools now to accomplish this goal—or any goal, for that matter, as long as it's aligned with my values!"

Dad chuckles a bit. "Ah, now you're starting to get it!"

As excited as I am to start on this goal, I remember we're still only halfway through Dad's ten-step series of life-changing skills. "So, what's our topic for tomorrow?" I ask.

"Tomorrow we'll discuss how to make better decisions. So today, I want you to list your top three values and the top three things you consider when making a decision. You'll probably have started thinking about some of these from examining your motivations for setting goals."

I scribble down my assignment. "This is very doable. Thanks, Dad. I love you!"

"Talk to you tomorrow morning, son. I love you, too!"

CHAPTER SIX

MAKING BETTER DECISIONS

Hmm, it seems like I'm waking up at the same time more often without the alarm going off. It's much nicer. And I like feeling excited about the day and looking forward to Dad's next letter.

Let's see, today's letter is about making decisions. My homework is to list my top three values and things I consider when making decisions. This'll be interesting, because yesterday's letter talked about values as part of goal setting.

Well, I know my top three values when making a decision are honesty, trust, and doing the right thing. And the top three things I consider are the pros, the cons, and whether my wife agrees.

With that in mind, I roll out of bed, get a quick shower, grab some coffee, and start reading.

Dear Son,

This letter will focus on how you can make better decisions and why that's important. Poor choices can lead to bad decisions. And every decision impacts your life.

Experts claim that your past decisions have pretty much formed who you are today. These decisions are also responsible for where you are at this point in life. So if you want to experience more happiness and more success in your future, you need to know how to make better decisions now.

As you know, decisions have consequences that can affect your family, friends, financial stability, reputation, and credibility, among other things. These consequences can have lasting impact and take a significant amount of time to remedy.

My mentor told me that making a better decision today can protect my reputation and help me avoid potential disasters tomorrow. He also said that if I do make a bad decision, I must be sure to learn the lesson of how and why it happened. Understanding a bad decision can help me strengthen my decision-making skills for the future.

If you feel your current decision-making strategies enable you to make good decisions, that's great. But remember, you can always learn new strategies to make even better decisions. It should be an ongoing learning process.

IMPORTANT AND UNIMPORTANT DECISIONS

Every day, we make many decisions. Some are unimportant, such as which shirt or blouse we should buy. These decisions often don't require much thought as they really don't impact our lives.

But we also make important decisions that do impact our lives, and they require more thought. For example, what type of career do you want? Where do you want to live? Do you rent or buy? What are the character traits, interests, values, and beliefs you're looking for in a spouse? Do you want children? If so, how many?

When you're faced with a decision, do you know whether it's unimportant or important? How do you recognize the difference? What strategies, if any, do you use?

And then the *most* profound decisions we make involve our spiritual life. Some examples: Will you accept Jesus as your Lord and Savior? Will Jesus be an important part of your daily life? Or will you only involve Him on Saturday or Sunday?

As I mentioned, important decisions need thoughtful consideration. We can approach that decision-making process in a number of ways. Perhaps the best way to approach it is by letting our values shape our decisions.

VALUES AND MAKING DECISIONS

Remember in my last letter how I talked about setting goals that aligned with your values? If a goal aligns with your values, it means it's important to you at a deep level of your being. It aligns with who you are or who you want to be. Therefore, you'll be more than likely to stay the course and achieve that goal.

Now I'm going to expand on the importance of values, because they are also a key factor in making important decisions. Put simply, knowing your values helps you make better decisions.

To help illustrate this, let's begin by having you list your values.

Identify and List Your Values

Why is it important to list your values? Because we need discipline to live by them. We need to remind ourselves continuously of our values so we can stay on track and be true to what is most important to us.

So, begin by listing all your values. Some examples include honesty, trust, dependability, loyalty, optimism, faithfulness, and so on. What qualities are important to you? Or perhaps it's easier to think of values as behaviors, such as being prompt, dressing neatly, or being kind to others.

As you make your list, think about where you get your values. As a general statement, people learn their values by watching family, friends, and society. Parents model the values they want their children to adopt. Because they instill values in their children through word and deed, they must be careful what they say and how they act.

Although many values come from the world around us, the best place to find our values is in God's Word. Unlike the ever-changing values obtained through society, God's values don't change. God's values remain the same yesterday, today, and tomorrow.

Which values on your list come from your family? Which come from society? Which come from God's Word? Thinking about the source of the values can help you identify what's truly important.

Negotiable Versus Nonnegotiable Values

Remember how there are important and unimportant decisions? Well, there are also negotiable and nonnegotiable values. Negotiable values are the ones you're willing to bend or even break if circumstances require. In contrast, nonnegotiable values are the ones you refuse to go against, regardless of the situation.

Go back through your list and identify which values are negotiable and which are nonnegotiable. How do you know? The key factor is: Does this value guide you in making important decisions?

An example of a negotiable value could be that you are always on time or always dress neatly when you leave the house. These can certainly be called values, strictly speaking.

But do they help you make important decisions in your life? Are they deeply meaningful values to you? Probably not. Is it OK to sometimes bend these values in certain situations? Probably.

Nonnegotiable values, on the other hand, must never be broken. They are absolutes that define your limits and guide you when faced with an important decision. They're a way of "being." You may remember the "be, do, have" approach I discussed in the letter yesterday.

To get you started, here are a few examples of nonnegotiable values you may already live by or that you may want to live by:

- Love God with all of your heart, soul, and mind, and love your neighbor as yourself.
- Live by God's Word. Love your family and help make them Christ-centered.
- Build solid family memories.
- Be trustworthy, honest, dependable, and disciplined.
- Do the right thing.
- Live by faith and not by emotions.
- Be committed to excellence in everything you do.
- Live a life of significance by making a difference in people's lives by helping, encouraging, and respecting them.
- Continue to grow in wisdom (mental), and in stature (physical), and in favor with God (spiritual) and man (social) (Luke 2:52).

Something as seemingly simple as listing your values and identifying the nonnegotiable ones can be a great tool for decision making. Say you're faced with a decision, and one of the choices is contrary to your nonnegotiable values. It's easy—you know you can't choose that option. Knowing your nonnegotiable values helps you determine your limits before you're confronted with the situation.

To say it another way, nonnegotiable values are like default answers to important decisions. It's impossible to predict all the challenges you'll face in your lifetime and decide how to handle them in advance. But knowing your nonnegotiable values makes it easier to make the right decisions as these challenges inevitably come up in life.

Once you're done making your list, keep it readily available so you can easily refer to it. Having a continuous reminder makes it less likely that your emotions will trump your rational thinking when you're in a crunch.

Strategies for Making Better Decisions

Jesus told us we all have a heart, soul, and mind (Matthew 22:37). As a strategy, we should use all three when we make a decision. For simplicity's sake, let's start with strategies for the soul, which I will call the spiritual factors. Next, we'll consider strategies for the mind, which I will call the analytical factors. And I'll conclude with strategies for the heart, which I call the physical factors.

Spiritual Factors

God asks that you involve Him in your decision making and asks us to seek Him first in everything we do (Matthew 6:33). In short, we are to first seek His kingdom and His righteousness.

God's kingdom is eternal. Is your decision consistent with His kingdom and the eternal things? As a reminder, the three eternals include God, His Word, and the people who will either spend eternity with Him or separated from Him. Is your decision consistent with His righteousness, which means doing what is right?

If you're ever tempted to make a decision contrary to your values, remember these two verses:

- " . . . and be sure your sin will find you out" (Numbers 32:23, RSV).

- "For what will it profit a man, if he gains the whole world and forfeits his life?" (Matthew 16:26, RSV).

In Proverbs 3:5–6, God promises to instruct us and teach us the way we should go. God will give us wisdom to make better decisions (James 1:5). All we have to do is ask for His help.

Ask Him now to give you wisdom, insight, and guidance so you can make better decisions. Do what King Solomon did: ask for an understanding mind and a discerning heart between right and wrong (1 Kings 3:9). In addition, specifically ask God to instruct, counsel, and teach you the way you should go (Psalm 32:8).

Analytical Factors

There are several steps to decision making from an analytical standpoint. Let's walk through each of them.

- **Information Gathering:** In order to consider your options, you need to gather information. This means determining what information you need, where you can you find it, and how reliable it is.

  You also need to check it for any biases—in the information itself and in your interpretation of it. Analyze closely. Is this information the truth? Or is it what *you* want to hear or what *they* want you to hear?

- **Cost:** As I said earlier in the chapter, decisions come with consequences. Jesus tells us to count the cost (Luke 14:28). What are the pros and cons for each choice, and what is the cost for each? What are you gaining (and at what cost)? What are you giving up (and at what cost)?

You need to think your decisions through to the end by asking what is likely to happen next if you choose one decision over another. Decide whether you can live with the consequences the different choices would bring.

- **Objectivity:** When you're in the analytical mode, you need to be objective and keep emotions out of it. Your grandfather told me that one way to separate myself from my emotions was to think about what advice I would give to someone contemplating the same decision.

  Another tactic—so long as you're not under a deadline—is to sleep on your decision. Whenever possible, don't rush into a decision, which can easily be colored by emotions and impulses. Instead, give yourself time to think about the pros and cons for a day to ensure that your emotions and biases are not affecting your decision.

  A little time can do wonders for your objectivity. You may be more emotionally invested in the outcome than you realize at first. But by morning, you may see it all in a different light.

- **Trusted Friend or Guide:** Sometimes it feels like we're all alone when it comes to decision making, but it doesn't need to be that way. Talk with a trusted friend. Ask them whether they have ever made a similar decision and what they learned. As you remember, your grandfather always told us to learn from the mistakes of others, because you can't live long enough to make all the mistakes yourself.

If you're lucky, maybe you have a Christian mentor who can help you make better decisions. My mentor Martin listens and acts as a "reality tester." When I don't realize I'm only focusing on *me*, Martin gives me a reality check and helps return my focus to Jesus. There are also times when, quite frankly, I don't feel like praying about an important decision. Martin's reality checks encourage me to continue.

Your mother has also helped me avoid making poor decisions. Between Martin and your mother, they have pointed out potential blind spots, traps, and land mines I wasn't able to see for myself at the time.

Physical Factors

When making your decision, pay attention to your body. What is your "heart" telling you? What is your "gut" telling you? Do you feel at peace, or do you feel anxious? Do you feel that your pending decision will provide you with additional energy or deplete it?

These physical signs are important factors to consider when making a decision. Often, our body gives us reality checks the same way a friend can. It's up to us to listen closely.

Have you ever had an uneasy stomachache that wouldn't go away until you made the right decision about an important issue? The instant relief confirms that you made the right call. If you make a decision and the stomachache remains, however, perhaps that's your body's way of telling you to reconsider.

Carrying It with You

The spiritual, analytical, and physical factors may seem like a lot to keep in mind when making a decision, especially if you're feeling stressed about it. Let me give you an easy way to remember the strategies above and carry them with you at all times.

Make a card with the information below and put it on your smartphone or in your wallet. It summarizes the steps you can take to align with your values and with God whenever you face a decision.

MAKING IMPORTANT DECISIONS

- Have I prayed for wisdom?
- Have I counted the cost, pros, and cons?
- Can I get input from Godly friends?
- Is this decision in accordance with my values?
- Is this decision in accordance with my goals?
- Is this decision in accordance with God's Word?
- Will it please God?
- Will it give me peace?

EXAMPLES OF GOOD DECISIONS BASED ON VALUES

Sometimes the best way to make value-based decisions is to consider how other people have made their decisions. Here are some examples from people you know from the Bible—and people you know from real life.

Joseph

Joseph's brothers threw him in a pit and sold him to strangers. Then one of Pharaoh's officials bought Joseph and entrusted him to run his household. Later, his wife tried to seduce Joseph. But Joseph had made a pre-decision not to sin against God (Genesis 39:9). It was a nonnegotiable value.

Joseph knew that we all face temptation. He also knew that we have a difficult time resisting that temptation if we don't have values to guide our decisions.

Paul

Paul made a decision to complete his mission to "testify to the gospel of the grace of God" regardless of the obstacles (Acts 20:24).

What obstacles did Paul face? Here are just a few: He was beaten and stoned multiple times. He spent many nights without sleep, food, and water. He was shipwrecked and in constant danger (2 Corinthians 11:23–28).

Did these obstacles stop Paul from carrying out his mission? The answer is no. He too had a nonnegotiable value that he would not break or bend under any conditions.

Your Sister

As you know, your sister played on an elite U-16 traveling soccer team. One night after a game, some girls considered renting an R-rated movie.

Your sister knew full well it was an inappropriate movie, seeing as they were all under seventeen. She told the other girls that if they rented the movie, she would go read a book in an adjacent room. Even though the team was adamant that she join them, she maintained her position. It was nonnegotiable, even under peer pressure.

Consequently, they decided to rent a PG-13 movie instead. Later, two of the girls thanked your sister for taking a stand. They too were uncomfortable with the R-rated movie, but they did not have the courage to stand up themselves.

Your sister shared this story with us after returning home. Your mom and I asked her how she was able to resist the peer pressure. She said she had made a pre-decision to live by her values—in particular, the value of honoring God and doing the right thing. She knew that if she hadn't decided on this nonnegotiable value in advance, she likely would have given in to the pressure, or her emotions would have overruled her thought process. She was glad that she remained firm for her own sake and also because it helped the other girls.

Your Grandfather
Now, I know I've talked a lot about the wisdom my father passed down to me. There's one bit he shared about making decisions that makes me smile every time I think of it.

Dad told me that when making a decision, I should consider three things: First, I should never confuse myself with someone "important." Second, I should remember that *not making* a decision is the same thing as *making* a decision. Third, I should remember that decision-makers can achieve desired outcomes, as long as they don't care who gets the credit.

Doesn't that make you smile too?

THE ONE THING
What's one thing that would help you make better decisions? Let's make this really simple: maybe it's to make the decision card I mentioned and put it in your smartphone.

I look forward to talking with you shortly—and I look forward to the next letter!

Love,
Dad

I take a deep breath. I'm smiling. Dad did it again. He's so amazing. What's really great is that he doesn't claim any credit for this wisdom. He's learned it from God's Word and from others who follow God's Word, and he's passing it on. I think about how lucky I am as I call Dad's number.

Dad picks up. "'Morning, son!" He sounds a little winded.

"Hi, Dad! How are you doing? You sound a little tired."

"Oh, I just had to hustle to find my phone, because I knew you'd be calling."

I'm not sure I believe his story. I wonder how he's really doing. I make a note to check in with Mom later.

"What did you think about the decision-making letter?" he asks.

"I loved this one, Dad! It gives me a lot of specific examples and steps to follow. I'm going to make up the card for Making Important Decisions. I'm going to list all my values, too. It's really helpful to think of them as negotiable and nonnegotiable. It makes things simpler. And for easy reference, I'm going to put my values and the decision-making steps on my smartphone."

Dad laughs. "I love hearing your enthusiasm! This is one of my favorite topics, too, because it shows such great ways to deal with life decisions as they come along."

I can't help but jump in. "Right—it's so practical!"

"Well, tomorrow's topic will be on managing problems. Your assignment is to write down one problem you're currently facing, then tell me how you're trying to manage it."

I write down the assignment. I've already got some ideas. Too many, in fact.

"OK, Dad. Got it!" I pause for a second, waiting. "You're going to take it easy today, right?"

Dad sighs a little. "Of course. I'm doing all the things your good mother and the doctor are telling me to do. I'm definitely taking it easy."

"Good," I say, feeling a bit better. "Thanks for telling me that. I'll look for that next letter and talk to you tomorrow. I love you, Dad!"

"Sounds good. Enjoy the rest of the day. Love you, too, son!"

CHAPTER SEVEN
MANAGING PROBLEMS

I open my eyes and look at the clock five minutes before the alarm goes off. Good. I like waking up on my own.

Dad's going to talk about managing problems today. I can feel a knot in the pit of my stomach. My problem is that I need to find a job. It's starting to really get to me.

I've used social media and my network to try to find something without any luck. I've had some leads, but nothing has panned out. I wonder if I'm doing something wrong. I can't think of what else to do so this topic is really timely. Maybe there will be some guidance in the letter. I sure hope so.

I take my shower and grab a coffee, then start reading Dad's letter.

Dear Son,

Today I will focus on the topic of managing problems. I say *problems*, but the following two additional words always come to mind: *tribulation* and *adversity*. So, let's start by reviewing how most dictionaries define these three words:

- **Problem:** A situation that presents doubt, uncertainty, difficulty, or discouragement.

- **Tribulation:** A sorrow or an unpleasant experience that in turn causes a problem that involves a difficulty, trouble, distress, or suffering.

- **Adversity:** A state of hardship or misfortune that tests one's faith and endurance.

When I was younger, I believed I was the only one who had difficult problems. It seemed as if all my friends were merrily going through life, free from problems. But I soon discovered they too had problems as difficult as mine.

I talked about problems in the second letter on peak performance and also in yesterday's letter on making better decisions. By now, you probably realize problems are a normal part of life. They're not necessarily *bad*, though. There is a reason for them.

My mentor Martin helped me understand the lessons we can learn from our problems. You see, problems help us mature, develop perseverance, and become closer to God. These happen because problems test us and force us to stretch ourselves outside our comfort zones. Without problems to make us stretch, there's a good chance we'd just stay right where we feel most comfortable. We'd miss out on personal and spiritual growth altogether.

When I talked of maintaining a positive attitude in the first letter, I reminded you that our problems, our battles, aren't against flesh and blood (the world). They're battles to fight spiritual attacks by the devil. Thankfully, though, God has provided us with spiritual weapons. God's Word says, "for the weapons of our warfare are not worldly but have divine power to destroy strongholds" (2 Corinthians 10:4, RSV).

Therefore, when facing problems, we need to use weapons that have divine power. With these weapons, we can create a plan to help reduce or even prevent some problems. We can also know how to better manage the problems that do come up.

USING SPIRITUAL WEAPONS TO REDUCE PROBLEMS

To prepare yourself for potential problems, each morning mentally put on the full armor of God (Ephesians 6:11–18). Two pieces of armor that are especially helpful in warding off problems are the shield of faith and the sword of the Spirit.

The shield of faith is a defensive weapon to stop the devil's "flaming arrows," which are the problems he shoots at you. Faith is the confident assurance that what you hope for will happen (Hebrews 11:1).

The sword of the Spirit is the Word of God. It's a powerful offensive weapon of guidance that is eternal and unchanging. God's Word is living and powerful (Hebrews 4:12).

Along with arming yourself with the shield of faith and the sword of the Spirit, you can also take actions throughout each day to reduce the number of problems you will encounter:

- Be alert. The devil's attack will come when you are vulnerable, such as when you feel lonely, unappreciated, and unhappy. Don't believe the rationalizations the devil sends to you when you're struggling with a problem. You might find yourself thinking, "It won't hurt anyone if I only do such-and-such just one time" or "It doesn't matter if I do such-and-such, because everyone else is doing it." These are lies. If your action would not please God, don't do it.

- Resist the devil by standing firm in your faith (1 Peter 5:9). Resistance can be a defensive action on our part to resist temptation such as avoiding certain situations. It can also be an offensive action such as using God's Word to resist the devil just as Jesus did when the devil tempted him in Matthew 4:1-11.

- Plug into Jesus, the power source (John 15:1–11). You do this by abiding in Him and keeping His commandments. To abide in Jesus means to have a close relationship with Him and to draw power from Him, much like a fish draws oxygen from water. When you are plugged into Jesus, you can ask for wisdom (James 1:5), supernatural power (Acts 1:8; Ephesians 3:20), and strength (Isaiah 40:31; 41:10).

- Live by faith and not by emotions (Galatians 2:20). Faith helps protect us from problems such as discouragement. Unlike emotions and feelings, which ebb and flow, faith is based on the eternal Word of God. Make your decisions based on the Word of God, and then act on it.

- Don't let the sun go down on your anger (Ephesians 4:26). God knows that if we don't deal with our anger before we go to bed, we can create emotional baggage that continues to build up. If you don't resolve these emotional issues they can explode unexpectedly, often weeks or months later with those you love.

- Each day, work with enthusiasm. Remember, you are working for the Lord rather than for a person (Colossians 3:23; Ephesians 6:7).

- Practice good time management, and keep uncommitted time in your life so you do not overload your capacity. You need to reserve some time each day so you have enough energy to handle unexpected problems as well as to rest, reflect, and strategize.

- Pray (1 Thessalonians 5:17). Every morning, start the day in prayer and continue to pray throughout the day.

HOW TO MANAGE PROBLEMS

You can see there are many things you can do to minimize the number of problems that come up in your life. But even if you plan well, you'll still have some problems. They can't be eliminated altogether.

Often problems have an emotional impact that makes them feel worse. Because of this, we don't operate at our best when faced with problems. We may fixate on only one aspect of the problem and can't see alternative solutions. Sometimes we get so focused on feeling sorry for ourselves that we can't think clearly about anything. We've all been there!

So what do you do when problems happen? Obviously, there isn't one solution to solve every problem. But there are ways to help you be in a better position to manage them.

Your attitude is a key factor. In the second letter, I listed God's blessings and promises to use in changing your attitude to ensure peak performance. In a similar way, your attitude is also very important in managing problems.

Here's a list of actions that you can take to cope with problems by focusing on the right thing—God!

- Ask God for help.
- Cast your problem on the Lord (Psalm 55:22).

- Cast your anxiety on Him (1 Peter 5:7).

- Keep your eyes on Jesus and not on your problem (Matthew 14:28–31; Isaiah 26:3).

- Don't run away. Face your problem in the name of the Lord.

- Be transformed by renewing your mind (Romans 12:2) by focusing on God's blessings and promises instead of your problems.

- If you caused the problem, ask for forgiveness (1 John 1:9).

- If someone has wronged you, forgive them (Mark 11:25; Matthew 6:14; 18:21–22; Colossians 3:13).

- Trust in the Lord and seek refuge in Him. God is a shield to those who take refuge in Him (Proverbs 30:5).

- God's Word tells us that if you trust in the Lord, you will not fear when heat comes, and you will not be anxious during difficult times (Jeremiah 17:7–8).

JIM'S STORY: MANAGING PROBLEMS BY FOCUSING ON GOD

I recently was able to help someone work through an emotionally distressing problem, and it's a good example of how to manage problems by focusing on God. The situation arose as a result of a friend's call for help. His son was deeply depressed because his girlfriend no longer wanted to date him. My friend was very concerned. He asked whether I would be willing to talk to his son, whom I'll call Jim (not his real name). Of course I was happy to help.

Jim listened grudgingly at first. He was very wrapped up in his loss and in feeling sorry for himself. I knew what he was feeling though. As I kept talking, I could see his body relax bit by bit. He even laughed a little when I mentioned one of his favorite movies. (Note that this was in the '90s!)

This is a summary of my conversation with Jim and my suggestions to help him cope with a loss that seemed impossible to deal with.

"Jim, your dad asked me to talk with you. I really do understand the pain you're feeling. I remember when I was in your same situation. My 'first love' told me she wanted to date other people. The pain was unbearable. At times, I thought I was going to die. It seemed endless. And just when I thought I was over it, the pain returned in waves that sometimes left me gasping for air. So please understand that your pain and emotions are not unusual. You are not alone in this.

"We all experience difficult, emotional problems in our lives," I continued. "But it's part of life. We all must figure out how to cope. Jesus doesn't tell us that if we're lucky, we won't face problems. Rather, Jesus tells us in John 16:33 that everyone *will* face problems. Everyone.

"God's Word tells us to cast our burden on Him and leave it there (Psalm 55:22). He will sustain you. You can pray something as simple as this: 'Dear Lord, my problem is too big for me to handle, so please help me. I ask for Your peace and Your direction by showing me how best to manage my problem.'

"God wants us to experience peace, and God's Word tells us what to do in order to achieve it. Namely, we need to keep our eyes and mind on Him and not on ourselves and our problems. The happy, successful person is better able to manage problems, because they reset their mind by shifting their focus. Instead of focusing on their problems, they focus instead on God's promises, such as all things work together for good to those who love the Lord.

"And that promise in Romans 8:28 is why I can confidently say that when God thinks the time is right, He will give you someone who is more amazing and loving than you could ever imagine. Right now, I know you think that seems impossible. But remember—all things are possible with God (Matthew 19:26).

"Your current problem can stop you temporarily, but only you can stop yourself permanently. Train yourself to be like the Terminator T-1000 in the *Terminator 2* movie. Every time someone or something knocked him down, he regrouped, jumped back on his feet, and resumed the battle.

"As difficult as it may be for you now, this problem is creating an opportunity for you to grow and mature. Even Jesus learned from His suffering (Hebrews 5:8).

God wants to make you better. So involve God in your problem. Ask for His help. Become better, not bitter. Use your current problem as a stepping stone to improve your relationship with the Lord. Ask God to help you stay focused on Him and His Word rather than focusing on your problem. Enjoy each day that God gives you, and don't forget to pray (1 Thessalonians 5:17). You have a bright and exciting future waiting for you!"

When I stopped talking, I was silent for a couple of minutes. Some big tears rolled down Jim's face. He was a little embarrassed. But he wiped at his eyes, took a deep breath, and nodded.

We all think we are so alone sometimes. It can be a revelation to hear that others have the same problems and that with God we are never alone.

We hugged, and I left.

I talked with my friend a couple of weeks later. He said Jim seemed to be getting back to his usual self. Jim had even joked around about them not getting enough pizza delivered for their usual Saturday night treat. A returning appetite is always a good sign!

Eleven years later, your mother and I attended Jim's wedding. He shared with me that I was right that God in His timing would give him someone more amazing and loving than he could ever have imagined!

As he and his bride walked down the aisle after the ceremony, I had an especially big smile on my face. And I looked up and said to myself, thank you Lord!

THE ONE THING

What is one thing you can do now to help better manage your problems? For example, maybe the one thing for you to do is to type up a list of God's blessings and put it on your smartphone. Remember that they were listed in my second letter. Then when a problem strikes, read God's blessings. His blessings will put your problem in the proper perspective, which in turn will help you manage it better.

Talk to you soon, son.

Dad

Things are really pulling together now. I'm starting to see how the letters are building on one another.

I grab a pen and paper for tomorrow's assignment, then call Dad.

"Hi, son!"

"Hi, Dad! Hey, I'm really starting to get how these lessons are building together. At least I think I am!" I laugh out loud, and Dad laughs back.

"OK," he says, "so tell me what you think you're 'getting.'"

"Well, you talked about God's blessings and promises—how that's from the letter on peak performance but also how it's a tool to manage problems. And living by faith and not by emotions was part of the letter on setting and achieving goals, and it shows up here too."

"I'm thrilled that you're paying such close attention. Yes, I believe you are getting it!"

"I haven't made a list of God's blessings and promises yet," I say. "I think I'll put them in my phone now, so I can look at them anytime I'm feeling, um, a little distressed . . ." My words trail off a bit.

Dad homes in on it immediately. "And what is the problem you identified for today's assignment?" he asks, already knowing the answer.

"Oh, the obvious one—finding a job!"

"I thought that was probably it." He pauses for a beat. "By the way, this is a good time to tell you I have a lead for you. One of my friends owns a small business near your house, and I just heard he's looking for a sales rep. If you're interested, I can send you his contact information."

"Dad, that's great!" I practically shout. "Yes, please!"

My head is spinning. A lead with one of Dad's friends. And it's for sales, which is what I've been hoping for. This might just be Romans 8:28 in action: all things work together for good to those who love the Lord.

"OK," he says. "I'll send that over and let him know you'll be in touch. And then it's up to you. In the meantime, I want you to start thinking about tomorrow's letter, which will be about managing worry, fear, anxiety, and stress."

I grab my pen, knowing the assignment is coming.

"Here are three questions to think about: What causes worry, fear, anxiety, and stress for you? What are the problems they in turn cause? And how do you deal with worry, fear, anxiety, and stress?"

As I jot this down, I get another knot in my stomach. Worry, fear, anxiety, and stress—I know this is a big one for me. But now that I've got some tools to manage problems better, maybe it will help with managing worry and stress as well.

I take a deep breath and know I can get through this. I hope Dad's letter tomorrow has some real gems for me, though.

"Got it, Dad. I'll be ready for your next letter tomorrow. And I'll let you know how it goes with your friend about the job!"

"Sounds good, son! I love you and good luck!"

CHAPTER EIGHT

MANAGING WORRY, FEAR, ANXIETY, AND STRESS

I'm awake earlier than normal, but I know it's because of the topic of Dad's letter today. What causes worry, fear, anxiety, and stress for me? What problems do they create, and how do I deal with them?

I deal with worry, fear, anxiety and stress every day, but I never thought about them as different things. They all feel the same to me: a big knot in my stomach. And yep, it's there now, just because I'm thinking about it.

I take a deep breath. Dad said not to let my emotions trump my rational thought. I'm going to focus on God instead. I take another deep breath and ask God to help me think clearly. *God, help me separate the big knot in my stomach into something that makes sense.*

OK, I know what my fears are: fear of failure, fear of rejection, and fear of the unknown. Good—I seem to be getting somewhere with this now.

What stresses me out? Having too many commitments and expectations.

What do I worry about? Everything! So many things could go wrong. What if they don't work out? What if everything falls apart?

Whenever I worry or feel fear, anxiety seems to follow right behind. It all makes me feel stressed out most of the time. I feel like I'm in a big loop going over the same things again and again with no way to get out of the cycle. It's exhausting.

What kind of problems come from this? I know it saps my energy. And I know for sure I've gotten sick from being drained by worry and stress. Sometimes I don't even realize I'm all balled up in it. When I do realize it, I try to shake it off with good things such as exercising or reading a book.

But I have to admit—sometimes I end up just indulging myself with binge-watching TV or eating or sleeping too much. Or I'll procrastinate and goof off surfing the internet just to give myself a "break" so I can forget about what's bothering me.

Yet the problem is always still there, waiting for me. It doesn't actually get better just because I wasted an hour watching funny dog videos.

I hope Dad can help me figure this out. It all seems like one big jumbled mess to me. Just thinking about this has me feeling pretty low.

I roll out of bed and force myself into the bathroom for a shower. That helps a little. I then go to the kitchen and have some coffee. I make a second cup this time before starting to read Dad's letter.

At last, I sit down at my desk, take another deep breath, and begin to read.

Dear Son,

This morning, I'm going to talk about worry, fear, anxiety, and stress. I'll look at how most dictionaries define them, talk a little bit about each, and list some ways to manage them. Then I'll provide guidance from the Bible on how God wants us to manage them.

- **Worry:** *Worry* can be a noun or a verb. As a noun, it's simply a thought that something bad may happen. As a verb, it's being afraid that something bad may happen.

- **Fear:** Like *worry*, *fear* can be both a noun and a verb. As a noun, it's an apprehensive emotion caused by a perceived present or future danger. When used as a verb, it's a response to an immediate and known threat.

- **Anxiety:** Anxiety is a feeling or response to a current or future stressor.

- **Stress:** Stress is our body's physical reaction to worry, anxiety, or fear.

ON THE POSITIVE SIDE

It's easy to think that all worry, fear, anxiety, and stress is bad. That isn't true in all cases. They all have positive aspects that can be helpful on many levels.

When it's a passing thought, worry can positively influence your decisions. It makes you consider the potential negative outcomes that may occur from your decisions. This can be very helpful in maintaining a balanced, rational perspective in your decision-making process.

Fear can also be useful. It helps us be alert to potential dangers. It sharpens our senses. It can also keep us safe if we need to react to an immediate threat.

Anxiety sometimes comes when we face a healthy challenge. It's a feeling that can be tinged with excitement. So the positive aspect of anxiety is that it can push us to stretch ourselves, to do something that exceeds what we think we are capable of doing. A little anxiety means we're pushing our comfort zone boundaries. And pushing those boundaries can keep us from becoming bored or apathetic.

A little stress is like a little anxiety. It can help us focus and perform better. Again, stress sometimes is mixed with excitement, and it can mean we're taking on a new challenge.

Often, stress isn't caused by external circumstances but our *internal response* to those circumstances. Your grandfather and brother are two people who have learned that. Unlike most people, they view stress as a friend who helps them rise to meet challenges.

Your grandfather confronts stress every day and every night, as he is the full-time caregiver for your grandmother, who you know has Alzheimer's. There's no downtime from Alzheimer's. Something unexpected could happen at any time, day or night.

But your grandfather thrives and performs his best when under pressure. He's always viewed stress as a friend. I once saw a T-shirt that summarizes his attitude. It read, "Good morning, let the stress begin." When I told him about it, he laughed and said the back should also read, "Good evening, let the stress begin." His attitude is what makes the difference.

Your brother is another example of someone who views stress as a positive. You may recall that he was the backup forward on his high school basketball team. During one game, the starting player got injured with only four seconds remaining in the game. With his team down by one point, your brother entered the game to replace his injured teammate.

I believe the other team underestimated your brother's ability to handle the pressure. After all, he had been sitting on the bench the whole game. He wasn't even warmed up! So, with just seconds left, a player on the other team fouled him to prevent a possible layup. The other team assumed he'd miss the free throws.

Your brother went to the free-throw line. Before he took his first shot, he glanced at your mother and me as we watched from the bleachers. He sunk his first shot and then the second to win the game. His teammates mobbed him.

After the game, your mother and I asked him why he looked over at us. He said it was because he was thinking about his grandfather, who taught him to view stress as a friend who would help him thrive under pressure. It was a lesson he obviously took to heart.

DISCERNING THE BALANCE

So now I've talked about worry, fear, anxiety, and stress as both positives and negatives. We've all experienced both sides. But how can we know the difference? Where do these emotions cross the line from positive to negative? How do we know when it's a good thing versus when it's something that needs to be managed?

Complicating everything is that these emotions can all feel the same. It can be difficult to know which emotion you're feeling at any given time, let alone whether it's positive or negative. If you don't know exactly what you're feeling, how can you manage it?

The one answer to all these questions isn't really that difficult: ask God for clarity. Listen to God's answer, and then listen to what's going through your heart, your body, and your mind.

Do you feel excited? Maybe you're having trouble sleeping—is it because you're happily playing out a million ideas on how something could work out? Or are you lying awake, counting all your problems, with your heart pumping and a growing feeling of dread?

But what do you do when you *know* you are deeply mired in the negative side?

HOW TO DEAL WITH EXCESSIVE WORRY, FEAR, ANXIETY AND STRESS

It can be pretty common to feel hopeless when you are consumed by worry, fear, anxiety, or stress. In that state of mind, it is difficult to know what to do. Remember your brother and grandfather, who both chose to view stress as a friend who helps them thrive under pressure. They chose their attitude, and it made all the difference. You can do this as well, especially once you better understand what you are really dealing with.

Worry

Worry is an activity of our choosing. When worry invades your thought life, you can choose to worry, or you can choose to trust God. The mind God gave us can't think about two things at the same time. You can't trust God and worry at the same time. So part of the answer to help manage worry is to trust God.

We also can't pray and worry at the same time. Consequently, God tells us to turn our worry into prayer. If you begin to worry, stop what you're doing and start praying.

Similarly, we can't think about Jesus and worry at the same time. God's Word tells us to keep our mind on Jesus, and we will experience His perfect peace (Isaiah 26:3).

Fear

Everyone is susceptible to a variety of fears, such as fear of failure, rejection, losing one's job, being alone, or death. You can think of fear as a storm. My mentor told me that every person is either in a storm, coming out of a storm, or about to enter one. It seems to be a cycle of life. What will you do when facing some type of storm in your life that causes you fear?

Jesus's disciples found themselves in this situation—quite literally. They were sailing across a lake when a strong storm rocked their boat so severely that it started to fill with water. The disciples were afraid they would drown, yet Jesus was sleeping peacefully in the stern.

The disciples woke Jesus and asked Him whether He cared if they perished (Mark 4:38). Jesus's answer was instructive: " . . . Why are you afraid? Have you no faith?" (Mark 4:40, RSV). Jesus specifically tells us, "fear not, for I am with you, be not dismayed, for I am your God; I will strengthen you, I will help you, I will uphold you with my victorious right hand" (Isaiah 41:10, RSV).

When storms strike, whom do you have in your boat to encourage you? If your fear level is high, that means your trust level in Jesus is low. So, increase your faith and trust in Jesus. He is always with us. He promised to never leave us or forsake us (Matthew 28:20; Hebrews 13:5–6).

Anxiety

God tells us that allowing anxiety to dominate our thought life is a waste because it can't add more time to our life (Luke 12:25–26). God's Word tells us: "Have no anxiety about anything, but in everything by prayer and supplication with thanksgiving let your requests be made known to God. And the peace of God, which passes all understanding, will keep your hearts and your minds in Christ Jesus" (Philippians 4:6–7, RSV).

Remember that anxiety is an emotion in response to something. Therefore, you need to identify what is causing you to be anxious. Are you worrying excessively? Are you afraid you won't be able to complete your responsibilities?

Are you unable to think clearly because of lack of sleep? Identifying why you are anxious is important. It allows you to address the root cause, rather than just the anxiety itself.

Stress

We know that stress is our body's reaction to worry, fear, and anxiety. We also know that too much stress can harm our health and can even shorten our life. It's important, then, to learn to manage this.

Because everyone is unique, what causes stress for me may energize you. Therefore, you need to identify what triggers these emotions in you. They can be events, workload, interactions with people, situations, expectations, and so on.

To help illustrate how these emotions build on each other, let me share a personal experience I had with stress and what caused it. It was a beautiful day to golf in Arizona. Your brother, cousin, and I had just teed off on a par three from the top of a hill that required a blind shot down to the pin on the green.

We jumped into our carts and headed for the green. As we rounded a sharp corner, we were suddenly confronted with a bobcat. He was crouching on all fours and staring at us.

My first reaction was to worry that something bad was about to happen, and I felt fear about the potential danger. And so I became anxious. My heart started pounding faster, and my breathing increased. This was my body's stress response to fear.

We slowed our carts. As we got closer, the bobcat relaxed and lounged on its side, as if to say he was no longer interested in us. And I too relaxed. I was no longer worried or afraid. Something bad didn't seem about to happen; there was no immediate threat.

That night, however, I heard on the news that a bobcat had attacked a golfer at the same golf course that day. My worry and anxiety returned. I obviously wasn't in danger at that moment watching the news. Rather, I was *anticipating* something bad happening tomorrow, when we planned to golf again.

As we rounded the blind corner at the same hole the next day, I became anxious from the worry and fear of the anticipated threat. But when the bobcat wasn't there, the worry and fear vanished. So did my anxiety.

The first scenario when we were face-to-face with the bobcat illustrates how my worry and fear created a physical response of anxiety and stress in my body. In the second scenario I only worried about *anticipating* a bad situation, which also triggered a physical response. This time it was anxiety. You can see how our response seems to take on a life of its own unless we actively choose to manage it.

STRATEGIES FOR MANAGING STRESS

By now you have a better understanding of how worry and fear can create anxiety and stress. Below are action steps you can take to better manage it all:

- Remember that your *internal response* to *external circumstances* creates worry, fear, and anxiety, which in turn causes a stress response from your body. In other words, no matter what happens externally, you have some measure of control over your stress level internally. You get to choose how you want to respond to situations. However, knowing this doesn't always make it easy. Ask God to transform your mind (Romans 12:2) to help manage your internal response to a particular stressor.

- When you identify what triggers your worry, fear, and anxiety, write it down. You can then create strategies to avoid triggers and better manage your stress levels. This is similar to identifying and overcoming obstacles, which I discussed in my fifth letter. Depending on your triggers, maybe a family member or friend can share with you how they manage theirs.

- Schedule time for relaxing during the day. Also, leave some uncommitted space in your life. This will give you an "emergency reserve" of time to handle the unexpected challenges that inevitably come up.

- Simplify your to-do list, and try to be realistic about how much time things can take. A common trigger for worry, fear, and anxiety is when you're rushing against a too-tight deadline.

- Deal with what is on your plate today, not tomorrow. If you're preoccupied with potential problems lurking in your future, your focus is diverted from what needs your attention now. Read Matthew 6:34, where God's Word tells us to focus on the problems that the current day presents and let those problems be sufficient for the day.

- Take care of your health. To manage stress, you need physical and emotional energy. Eat a balanced diet and exercise.

- Get adequate sleep. This is essential. If you don't, even trivial things can be stressful. As General George S. Patton once said, "Fatigue makes cowards of us all."

- Try to maintain a positive attitude. I say "try" because even though there is so much to be thankful for, it can still be a struggle to maintain a positive attitude. Trying with your whole heart every day is most important. It'll get easier, though, as it becomes a habit. One way to do this is to start the day off right with an attitude of gratitude. Here is a pertinent verse that you can recite each morning: "This is the day which the LORD has made; let us rejoice and be glad in it" (Psalm 118:24, RSV).

WHAT TO DO WHEN YOU STILL CAN'T MANAGE WORRY, FEAR, ANXIETY, AND STRESS

Even though you may take preventative steps to reduce worry, fear, anxiety, and stress, these problems occasionally penetrate even the best defenses. When they do, follow the checklist from 2 Chronicles 20:1–23 to help you manage them.

The Bible tells the story of a man who followed God's Word when under great pressure. His name was Jehoshaphat, and he was once king of Judah. Because he obeyed God's commandments, God was with him (2 Chronicles 17:3–4).

But one day, three tribes prepared to wage war against Judah. Some of Jehoshaphat's men reported, "A great multitude is coming against you" (2 Chronicles 20:2, RSV). The armies from the nations that were about to attack were more powerful than his.

Instead of being consumed by his worry, fear, anxiety, and stress, Jehoshaphat took nine action steps, and his enemies were overpowered. These actions are recorded in 2 Chronicles 20:

1. He didn't run from the worry, fear, anxiety, and stress.
2. He prayed and fasted (v. 3, 18).
3. He asked God what to do and asked for His help (v. 3–4).
4. He did what God told him to do.
5. He stood firm in his faith (v. 5–6).
6. He praised God (v. 19).

7. He believed in the Lord (v. 20).
8. He gave thanks to God (v. 21).
9. He sang and gave praise to God (v. 21).

The good news is, if we too act on these nine steps, we no longer have to fear. God's Word tells us that He takes over and fights the battle for us (v. 15).

GOD'S WILL VERSUS OUR WANTS

Even though God's Word tells us to trust Him at all times (Psalm 62:8), and even though God's Word tells us that He honors those who honor Him (1 Samuel 2:30), we must understand that He may not always give us what we ask for. I admit there have been times when I wanted something now, not later. But should I always receive what I want, when I want it? We need to trust God to provide in His timing. God wants the very best for us, but that may result in a different outcome from what we think it should be.

Consider how many times life has turned out in a way you didn't like. You may have even raged at God and asked why something happened—only to later realize that the situation resulted in a very valuable lesson or an amazing opportunity.

Remember my friend's son Jim in the last letter? Jim eventually became very grateful for that breakup he experienced as a younger man. Otherwise, he never would have met and then married his amazing bride eleven years later.

We need to have faith in God's will and trust that the outcomes will always be for our highest good. But regardless of the outcome, you must decide who you are going to trust and serve. Will it be yourself? Will it be society? Or will it be God?

When we built our first home many years ago, your mom made that decision for our family. As you entered the front door, the first thing you saw was a sign that read, " . . . but as for me and my house, we will serve the LORD" (Joshua 24:15, RSV).

THE ONE THING

What is one thing that you can do now to manage worry, fear, anxiety, and stress? For example, maybe you will make a conscious decision to put your trust in God and ask Him to help you. Perhaps you could make a sign for your home.

I wish you all the best,

Dad

Once again, I let out a deep breath. Actually, it's a sigh of relief. I just need to ask God for help and trust that the outcome will be for the best. It's that easy.

Still, I know this will be an exercise in letting go. I usually want life to go a certain way, and when it doesn't, I spiral down. When really, life should go *God's* way, not mine. Looking back on some of my stress points, I realize they didn't need to be there at all, had I only had the right mind-set.

I fumble kind of absentmindedly for a pen and paper while I dial up Dad. I accidentally mess up the number and have to try it again. I guess I'm still a little preoccupied, thinking about all those stressors that I've been carrying around.

Dad answers on the first ring. "Hi, son!"

"Hey, Dad . . ." I don't say anything else.

After a few seconds, Dad says, "So, I think I can hear the wheels turning in your head. Did this one give you a lot to think about?"

"I'll say!" I finally reply. "I'm sitting here thinking about all the times I've gotten all stressed out over things that weren't even real issues. I'm too focused on what I want and the way I think things need to be. I never realized that God's got this! All I've needed to do was let go and focus on Him. I feel kind of dumb now." I'm out of words again.

"Son, this is not about beating yourself up," he says gently. "So you're realizing some things about yourself that you didn't know before. That is called growth, and it's a wonderful thing! You should be overjoyed about it. I know I am! And besides, this growth comes with important lessons. Think of it this way: You wanted to find a new job right away, right? But if life had gone the way you wanted, do you think we would be having these daily chats about following God's Word?"

This hits me right between the eyes. The lesson has been there the whole time. I keep seeing being jobless as this awful situation. When really, it's God's way of giving me an opportunity to have a closer relationship with Him. And also with my dad.

My eyes start tearing up. The knot in my stomach is gone. Now I know why I've been so anxious about today's topic. I must have sensed there was an important lesson I needed to learn about myself, but I didn't want to face it.

Now I'm glad I did. Really glad.

"Thank you for saying that, Dad. This is so amazing."

I'm out of words again. I don't want Dad to know I'm crying. I think he can tell, but he saves me by moving right on.

"So, now, I want to talk about tomorrow's assignment. As I mentioned, I'm going to discuss time management. I think you'll appreciate how well it works in tandem with today's information. It's more task-oriented, and I think you'll like that. Before tomorrow, I want you to do some homework: First, list one action you could take to manage your time better. Second, ponder this question: How does God want you to spend your time? Got those?"

"Yes, Dad, I do!" I'm feeling so relieved, lighter. I already know this next letter will help a lot too.

"Excellent! Then I'll let you get on with your day. Let me know when you hear back about that job opportunity with my friend!"

"You will be the first to know!" I say. "Love you!

CHAPTER NINE

MANAGING TIME

I'm not feeling anxious about today's topic on time management. I feel like I'm in somewhat familiar territory on this one. I've been to a number of workshops on effective time management. That's not to say I *excel* at time management, but just that I kind of know what to expect from this letter.

Well . . . at least I think I do. I am pretty curious to hear what Dad has to say. He's given many presentations on time management from a business standpoint, but this is different. His letters surprise me every time, so maybe I better hold off on any expectations.

Before I can begin reading, I need to answer those two questions.

What's one action that I could take to manage my time better? Maybe I could end each night by making a list of things I want to accomplish the next day.

How does God want me to spend my time? I think God wants me to find time to help and encourage others in addition to the time I spend at work and with my family.

With my homework done, I dive into the routine I've followed since the very first letter: I shower, grab a coffee, sit at my desk, and start to read.

Dear Son,

We all have days when time just seems to slip through our fingers. But if you end every day wondering why you didn't accomplish much, and if you often feel a lack of control in your life, you're probably not managing time effectively.

In today's world, there's a constant demand for our time and attention. Things seem to keep speeding up, commitments are always growing, and pressure keeps mounting to do more at work, at home, and in the community. It's very easy to get caught up in trying to do everything. Oftentimes, it's very difficult to know what to even do first.

If you want to gain more control over your life and live it according to God's Word, you need to know how to manage your time—otherwise, your time will manage you.

In this letter, I'll discuss why it's important to manage time, how God wants us to use our time, and how we can use our time more effectively. Your homework for this topic will be a little different, though. It'll be a weeklong study on how you spend your time. I'll describe how that works later in the letter.

But first, let's explore why time management is an important life skill not just in a secular sense but more importantly in a spiritual sense.

EIGHT FACTS ABOUT TIME

What does God's Word tell us about time? These eight facts set the record straight.

1. **Life on earth is short.** " . . . What is your life? For you are a mist that appears for a little time and then vanishes" (James 4:14, RSV). In the common era, the oldest woman

in the world lived 122 years and 164 days. The oldest man lived 116 years and 54 days. But even if you live 122 years, this is miniscule compared to your eternal life.

2. **Earth is not our home.** We are sojourners as we reside temporarily on earth (1 Chronicles 29:15). Our home is in heaven. (Philippians 3:20).

3. **We are going to die.** " . . . it is appointed for men to die once . . . " (Hebrews 9:27, RSV).

4. **After we die, we face judgment.** "And just as it is appointed for men to die once, and after that comes judgment" (Hebrews 9:27, RSV).

5. **We will appear before God.** Every person will give an account to God (Romans 14:12), and He will repay us for what we have done (Matthew 16:27; 2 Corinthians 5:10).

6. **We will either be with God or separated from Him for eternity.** After we die and appear at the judgment seat, God's Word tells us that we will either live with God or be separated from Him (1 John 5:11–13).

7. **After we die, nothing material leaves the earth with us.** God's Word tells us, "for we brought nothing into the world, and we cannot take anything out of the world" (1 Timothy 6:7, RSV).

8. **When we are in heaven, the three eternals will be with us.** As a reminder from the first letter, there are only three eternals: God, His Word, and people.

Time is one of our most precious resources from God. We get only twenty-four hours in a day to do whatever we want to accomplish. We can't get more.

Read facts number three, five, and seven again. We will die. We have to account for our life to God. And we must leave all material treasures behind. Is it clear now why we need to manage time? We don't get a "do-over" if we mismanage our time in this life and spend it the wrong way. And judgment in heaven does not give points for good intentions or big bank accounts!

Yet many people squander their precious time. They work endlessly just so they can amass treasures and toys, as though they will live on this earth forever. They may *say* their priority is spiritual development, but the way they spend their time proves otherwise. Their actions speak much louder than their words.

How much time do *you* spend preparing for eternal life? Consider how you spend your time. What do your choices say about your *true* priorities versus what you're *saying* are your priorities? This is the real question. Only you and God know the answer.

The reason we need to manage our time is so we can spend it on what's important in God's eyes. If our time manages us, it will let the influences of the world make those choices for us. It takes effort to focus on the right things and to use time, this precious resource, as God intended.

I believe God wants everyone to understand what's really important (Psalm 90:12). That's why He tells us to make the most of our limited time while we're on earth (Ephesians 5:15–16).

LIVING THE BASICS

How do you think God would have us spend each day? God has two desires: First, He wants us to spend some time doing what He created us to do. Second, He wants us to spend some time preparing for our eternal life in heaven. We can accomplish His two desires by returning to the basics.

Here are a few basics God wants you to follow while you live on earth and prepare for eternity:

- God requires that we do justice, love kindness, and walk humbly with Him (Micah 6:8). To do justice, we must do what is right. To love kindness, we must love people. And God's Word tells us what love is and what it is not. For example, "Love is patient and kind; love is not jealous or boastful; it is not arrogant or rude. Love does not insist on its own way; it is not irritable or resentful; it does not rejoice at wrong, but rejoices in the right. Love bears all things, believes all things, hopes all things, endures all things" (1 Corinthians 13:4–7, RSV).

- God created us in Christ Jesus to do good works (Ephesians 2:10). Son, your mom is a good example of someone who consistently does good works. When she sees a need, she cheerfully steps in and helps, whether that means providing a hot meal for someone who is sick or providing encouragement to someone who is discouraged. She loves people and regularly prays for them and with them.

- God wants us to maintain an eternal perspective. God tells us, "Set your minds on things that are above, not on things that are on earth" (Colossians 3:2, RSV).

Before you can manage your time according to God's Word, you need to determine how you're currently spending your time. The best way to do this is to conduct your own personal time study—which is the homework I mentioned earlier. Let's look now at how this works.

TIME STUDY

In a time study, you track your activities in fifteen-minute segments for one week—Monday morning to Sunday night. This exercise will help you see how you actually spend your time. More importantly, it helps you see whether you're spending your time on the right things.

Before I go into detail about how to do a time study, let me offer some advice: have the courage to be honest with yourself during your time study. You will find it much more beneficial if you do.

In the end, your time study will show you segments of "lost" or "wasted" time. You'll begin to see the impact it has on your day. It'll also show any disparity between your proclaimed priorities and your actual priorities.

For this reason, you might be tempted to change up your normal routine when doing the study. For example, if you never spend time reading the Bible each day, you might feel the urge to do it now, just to make your time study look "better."

This is where honesty comes in. To get the most out of this exercise, you need to accurately track how you typically spend your time, for better or worse. So don't start doing something that you don't already do on a regular basis.

Remind yourself that *conducting* the time study is one step and *analyzing* it is another. Changes shouldn't happen during the conducting step. That's merely when you record how you spend your time—no judgments, no changes. Afterward, you'll have the chance to closely analyze the results. That's when you can decide whether and where you may need to make changes.

The time study will examine your life in fifteen-minute segments. Let's zoom in on why.

Your Life—Fifteen Minutes at a Time

Most of us would say our lives naturally break into fifteen-minute segments. It's a manageable amount of time for even a simple task. For instance, we can easily take fifteen minutes just getting a cup of coffee and chatting with a colleague at work. We can take fifteen minutes to answer an email or get a snack.

Do you know how many fifteen-minute segments you have in each day? Ninety-six. The image below represents a single day divided into these ninety-six segments. It helps put into perspective just how much time we *really* have.

So now let's figure out how you're spending that time. What do you do with your ninety-six fifteen-minute segments?

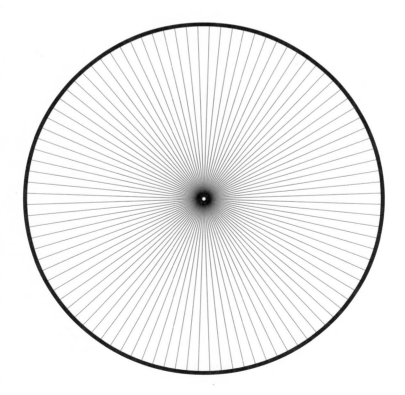

Conduct Your Time Study

Plan to start your time study on a Monday morning. In the meantime, though, make sure you have everything in place. One way to track your time is to set the timer feature on your phone to alert you every 15 minutes. You'll also need your phone or a notepad and pen to record your data. Whatever format you use, make sure you can easily transfer or work with the data later.

If you decide to go the timer route, keep the timer with you throughout the entire week, beginning first thing Monday morning. (Yes, you can turn it off at night, so long as you record the time when you go to bed and when you wake up.) Each time the timer alerts you, jot down what you've been doing during those fifteen minutes. Don't forget to include the preparation time that goes with each activity, such as the time it takes to prep a meal, get ready for bed, or commute to work.

It may seem like a hassle to keep jotting down your activities every fifteen minutes for an entire week. But it's important to record your time as you spend it, rather than wait to fill out your study at the end of the day, when your memories are no doubt hazy. If you could remember how you spent each of your time segments, you probably wouldn't need to do a time study!

Not to mention, recording your activities every fifteen minutes will provide the most accurate results. We often don't have a clear sense of how long we spent on a single activity. We may think we spent fifteen minutes checking sports scores, when actually, we zoned out for three times that long.

Analyze Your Time Study

After you complete your weeklong time study, the next step is to analyze its results. You may want to transfer your data into a chart, graph, spreadsheet, color-coded list—whatever best suits you. This step can be as simple or as complex as you'd like.

Begin by grouping your activities into categories. To get you started, here are some general categories, but you can tweak them as needed. Note that some activities may fall into more than one category, such as going for a bike ride with your kids.

- Career
- Family
- Spiritual
- Exercise
- Household maintenance and chores
- Financial tasks and paying bills
- Leisure/recreation/socializing/hobbies
- Meals/eating
- Screen time/technology etc.
- Sleeping

After you've grouped a week's worth of activities, spend some time studying the groupings and tallying how much time you spent in each. Then ask yourself what you've learned about yourself.

What categories are biggest? Which are smallest? Do you think your time is appropriately balanced between your true priorities and less-important activities? Are you spending quality and quantity time equally with your kids? Are you keeping in touch with extended family or friends?

Did you work late or take work home—because you take a lot of unnecessary breaks during the actual workday? Did you pass up a morning church service—because you stayed up late binge-watching a TV show the night before?

Now that you've conducted and analyzed your time study, ask yourself what, if any, corrective steps you need to take. In particular, think about how God wants you to spend your time.

MAKING TIME FOR GOD

There are many techniques for managing your time. Most are secular task-oriented strategies that help you better prioritize, avoid procrastination, stay focused, and so on.

However, the most important time-management technique is generally not even considered a technique. It's simply spending time with God, every day.

When you spend time with God each day, you refresh, recharge, and gain access to His resources, including His wisdom, insight, guidance, and supernatural power. And if you choose to ask for and use God's resources in your time-management decisions, He'll not only help you leverage your time but He'll also provide you the ability and power to enjoy a happier and more significant life.

Psalm 84:10 (RSV) states, "For a day in thy courts is better than a thousand elsewhere . . . " In other words, spending one day with God is more beneficial than spending a thousand days elsewhere.

As lovely as it sounds, who can realistically spend the entire day with God? A time study is proof that we have jobs, families, and lives God wants us to live to our fullest.

How about spending one hour with God each day, then? If we extrapolate the Psalm verse, we could argue that spending one hour with God each day is more beneficial than spending a thousand hours elsewhere.

And yet, few people are willing or able to spend even one hour with God each day. Especially when you're working full-time and raising an active family, it's difficult to find a solid hour of free time. Looking at your time study, you likely won't see a whole hour of uninterrupted time every day.

So let's be realistic: How about spending just *fifteen minutes* with God each day? Many people may still balk at this. When time manages us, we feel harried, rushed, and so busy that the idea of setting aside even fifteen minutes seems impossible.

This is why time management is so important. In order to live our best life according to God's Word, we must ensure we have time every day to devote to Him—even if it's just one of those ninety-six fifteen-minute segments.

Compared to spending an entire day or hour with God, fifteen minutes may not seem like much. But if we once again extrapolate on Psalm 84:10, we could argue that spending one fifteen-minute segment with God is more beneficial than spending a thousand fifteen-minute segments elsewhere.

If we do the math, one thousand fifteen-minute segments equals 250 hours. In other words, fifteen minutes with God is better than 250 hours spent on your own power. I consider an investment of fifteen minutes to 250 hours a pretty good return!

So, take a look at your time study. Can you identify which fifteen-minute segment you will spend with God every day? It might be easy: you might see that every morning, you have fifteen minutes of quiet time to yourself before the kids wake up.

If it isn't easy to find fifteen minutes for your spiritual life, then it likely means you need to make some changes in your secular life. For instance, could those fifteen minutes of mindless channel surfing before supper turn into time with God instead? Or what about those fifteen minutes you spend every night before bed, checking emails and fretting about the next day's work? To avoid this, perhaps you could make a to-do list before you leave work, so you know three things you want to accomplish the next day.

Look at your time study and then look again at that image of the ninety-six segments. Do whatever it takes to devote one of those segments to God.

THE ONE THING

In a short period of time, we have covered a lot of material on how to become a better time manager. So, what is one thing you can do today to help you manage your time better—in the secular sense but more importantly in the spiritual sense?

Naturally, the best place to start is to identify how you can leverage your time by spending at least fifteen minutes with God every day and gain access to His resources.

I wish you the best!

Dad

I can't help but laugh out loud. This is very cool! Dad was right about me liking this topic.

I for sure plan to do the time study. But even without the study, I already know how many time wasters make up my day. I always think I have a "good" reason for them. For instance, I tell myself that channel surfing relieves stress. Yet then I'm surprised and frustrated when I run out of time each day to do the things I really should be doing.

Even over the past nine days, I've struggled to find time to do the spiritual activities we've been discussing in the letters. No wonder that happens!

I call Dad. I'm still shaking my head in disbelief at myself when he answers.

"Hi, son!"

"Hi, Dad! Yep, you were right—again! This was a great topic for me. I've learned so much, even before I do a time study."

I pause to gather my thoughts. "You know, I'm really glad we didn't start with this letter on time management. It's only now, after having gone through the other letters, can I understand why managing my time is so important. I realize now why I need to better manage my time so I can dedicate it to the *most* important thing in my life—my spiritual growth."

"It's pure joy to hear you say that," Dad replies.

There's another pause. I'm grinning, and I'm pretty sure Dad is too.

Finally, he breaks the silence. "So, now let's talk about what's coming up in the last letter."

I grab a pen and paper. "OK, shoot!"

"I'll discuss creating and maintaining a powerful prayer life. Even though this is the last of the ten life-changing skills, many believe establishing a prayer life is the single most important skill to learn and apply. Your homework is to think about these two questions: First, what is one thing you could do right now to improve your prayer life? Second, what is one hindrance to your prayer life? Got it?"

"Yes! Got it!"

"OK, son. I'll let you get on with your day. Sun's shining. It should be gorgeous!"

"Thanks so much for your help, Dad. I'll talk to you tomorrow. Love you!"

"Love you too."

CHAPTER TEN

CREATING AND MAINTAINING A POWERFUL PRAYER LIFE

My eyes fly open before the alarm goes off. I can't believe this is the last letter about the ten life-changing skills. It doesn't seem possible. I still have so much to learn! But I totally trust Dad and his process, so I'll just go with it.

Dad said that prayer may be the most important life-changing skill to learn and use, so I'm going to spend extra time answering his last two questions.

OK, question one: What can I do to improve my prayer life right now? Well, for one, pray more. I seem to pray only when I'm desperate, but that doesn't line up at all with what Dad has been sharing. Aside from that, I think the most important thing I can do is figure out how to get plugged into Jesus and stay plugged into Him. I have no doubt that Dad can help me revitalize and empower my prayer life.

And question two is: What's one hindrance to my prayer life? I know I haven't been honest with God or myself about my sins. I try to pretend I haven't sinned, but the truth eats at me. Maybe unconfessed sin is a hindrance to prayer.

I roll out of bed and walk into the kitchen to make coffee. I find myself putzing a bit, out of my usual routine. I know I'm stalling, trying to stretch this moment. I don't really want these letters and daily chats with Dad to end.

Then I suddenly realize there's no reason they need to end. I don't need the excuse of going over a daily letter to call my dad! I'm going to connect with Dad a whole lot more often from now on. Besides, I know I'll need continuing support to help me incorporate these new life skills.

With that, I'm ready to take my shower. I then grab my coffee, sit down at my desk, and start to read. I feel very calm.

Dear Son,

Today, it's all about your prayer life. To help set the tone, let me go back a few years to the time when I began to understand how important prayer is.

When I was in college, your grandfather told me that I should pray to God in the name of His Son, Jesus Christ, and in the power of the Holy Spirit. The idea of going straight to God with my prayers was kind of intimidating for me, though. How could I, a mere human, gain access to God?

Initially, I assumed there were several ways to gain access. But when I skimmed the New Testament, I found there is only one way: God's Word tells us that we have access to God through Jesus (Ephesians 2:18). I also read, "Jesus said to him, 'I am the way, and the truth, and the life; no one comes to the Father, but by me'" (John 14:6, RSV). I noted that Jesus did not say He is just one of several possible ways to gain access to God. Instead, Jesus said He is the *only* way.

Of course, that led to my next question: If Jesus is the only way to gain access to God, then how could I gain access to Jesus? I found a verse that said, "For God so loved the world that he gave his only Son, that whoever believes in him should not perish but have eternal life" (John 3:16, RSV).

I thought that meant all I had to do was believe that Jesus is God's Son to get that access. But then I read that even the demons believe that Jesus is God's Son (James 2:19). Yet the demons do not have access to Jesus. Simple belief is not enough. You may remember this same idea in the "Becoming a Believer" letter I sent that day you came to visit us.

When I pressed on, I found the answer in two verses of God's Word: One, "because, if you confess with your lips that Jesus is Lord and believe in your heart that God raised him from the dead, you will be saved" (Romans 10:9, RSV). And two, "Behold, I stand at the door and knock; if any one hears my voice and opens the door, I will come in to him and eat with him, and he with me" (Revelation 3:20, RSV).

These verses taught me what I must do. In short, I needed to do three things the demons failed to do: to confess in my heart that Jesus is Lord and that God raised Him from the dead; to receive Jesus by asking Him to come into my life as Lord and Savior; and to continue to know Jesus by maintaining a daily relationship with Him.

And prayer is how we maintain that relationship by communicating with Him throughout the day. This is why it's the most important life skill of them all.

UNDERSTANDING PRAYER

We often talk about prayer without understanding it very well. We all know we should pray, but we may not understand why it's important or even how to do it. So I want to go over some basics that'll make sure you and I are talking about the same thing.

What Prayer Is
In the simplest terms, prayer is talking with God.

Why It's Important to Pray
We pray to create and maintain a relationship with the Holy Trinity. God is near to all who call upon Him (Psalm 145:18). When we die, we don't want Jesus to tell us to depart because He never knew us (Matthew 7:23).

We also pray to obtain wisdom. God's Word tells us to obtain wisdom (Proverbs 4:5). Wisdom is more valuable than jewels (Proverbs 8:11) and gold (Proverbs 16:16). Thankfully, all we have to do is ask God for wisdom, and He will give it to us (James 1:5).

In addition to obtaining wisdom, prayer helps us receive insight and guidance (Proverbs 3:5, 6). God's Word also says, "Call to me and I will answer you, and will tell you great and hidden things which you have not known" (Jeremiah 33:3, RSV).

Not to mention that prayer helps recharge and revitalize our life (Psalm 23:3; Isaiah 40:31; and Acts 3:19).

When and Where to Pray
While I was typing material for a presentation on prayer, my computer crashed. I discovered that a construction company in the neighborhood accidentally cut the fiber-optic line servicing the homes on our block. During the time that the construction crews were fixing the line, I had no access to my computer.

But the good news for us is that when it comes to praying, God is always available. Therefore, we can pray anywhere and anytime without worrying about experiencing a disconnect or downtime.

God's Word tells us to develop the habit of praying throughout the day (1 Thessalonians 5:17). This means prayer isn't something you do only before meals and at bedtime. Prayer can and should happen all day long. Personally, I pray for wisdom, guidance, and insight before meetings, phone calls, and writing. I also like to pray while I'm driving, waiting in lines, and walking. My mentor Martin enjoys swimming laps every day, and he prays for a different person during each lap.

So don't say you don't have time to pray. As I discussed in the fourth letter about maintaining balance, we *always* find time to do what we want to do.

Different Ways to Pray

Some people find themselves not praying simply because they worry they'll do it "wrong." Actually, there are several ways to pray.

To start, you can use the model prayer that Jesus gave his disciples that we call the Lord's Prayer. Jesus told his disciples, "Pray then like this:

> *Our Father who art in heaven, Hallowed be thy name. Thy kingdom come, Thy will be done, On earth as it is in heaven. Give us this day our daily bread; And forgive us our debts, As we also have forgiven our debtors. And lead us not into temptation, But deliver us from evil." (Matthew 6:9–13, RSV). For thine is the kingdom and the power and the glory, forever.* (Other authorities add this last sentence.) *Amen.*

You can create your own prayer as well, of course. As a guide, include these elements:

- **Confession:** Our sins hide God's face from us so that He does not hear (Isaiah 59:2). Therefore, if we want God to hear our prayer, we need to confess our sins and seek His forgiveness. As a prelude to each prayer, ask God to search you and know your heart to bring any sin to light (Psalm 139:23, 24).

- **Adoration:** Begin your prayer by praising Him. "Great is the Lord and greatly to be praised . . . " (Psalm 48:1, RSV).

- **Thanksgiving:** Examine your life—you have a lot to be thankful for, including God's promises and blessings, which we discussed in chapter 2. Let us remember the story of the ten lepers. Jesus healed them all, yet only one leper gave thanks after this miracle. To this, Jesus replied, " . . . Were not ten cleansed? Where are the nine?" (Luke 17:17, RSV). When you pray, don't be like the nine lepers. Rather, be like the one who gave God thanks.

- **Supplication:** Supplication means asking God for something. If you want to receive something from God, you need to ask (Matthew 7:7–8). If you feel you aren't receiving the things you want, it may be because you haven't actually asked (James 4:2). Then again, it may also be because you have asked for the wrong reason (James 4:3). This is where God's wisdom can help us. (We'll explore these points later in the letter.)

- **Intercession:** Asking God for something on someone else's behalf is called intercession. Son, your mom is a model for intercessory prayer. Every morning, she prays for our family. As your mom might tell you, it's helpful to find out someone's specific need so you can pray more specifically for them. You can then pray for them with a verse from God's Word that meets their need. And if you find yourself talking to someone who tells you about a problem, pray for them right then and there.

PRAY WITH MORE POWER

Now that you know what prayer is and how to do it, it's time to learn how to deepen your prayer life. The deeper you go, the more power you can experience in your prayer. Here are some ways to "power up" your prayer life.

Abide in Jesus

Do you remember when Mom and I visited your brother in Japan when he was working for a company that produced wine? The owner gave us a tour of his vineyard. He explained he takes great care to ensure that the vines remain connected to the branches so that sap (nourishment) from the vines continually flows through the branches to produce the fruit.

Jesus also uses the analogy of the vineyard, with the vines connected to the branches to draw nourishment. Likewise, we must remain connected to Him in order to receive His nourishment so that we can produce eternal fruit. Jesus said, " . . . Abide in me, and I in you. As the branch cannot bear fruit by itself, unless it abides in the vine, neither can you, unless you abide in me. I am the vine, you are the branches. He who abides in me, and I in him, he it is that bears much fruit, for apart from me you can do nothing" (John 15:4–5, RSV).

If we keep God's commandments and do what pleases Him, we abide in Jesus, and He abides in us (John 15:10). Also, we abide in Jesus if we confess that Jesus is the Son of God (1 John 4:15).

When you abide in Jesus, you come to God in the name of His Son. As stated earlier in the letter, Jesus said that no one can come to the Father but by Him (John 14:6). This is why I can't emphasize enough how important it is for you to plug into Jesus and stay connected.

Therefore, check throughout the day to ensure that you do not loosen or break your connection. Ask yourself whether you did something during the day that did not please God.

Pray in the Spirit

God realizes that we don't always know what to pray for or how to pray. This is why God's Word tells us to pray at all times in the Spirit, because the Holy Spirit will guide and direct our prayers (Ephesians 6:18).

So, remember to start each day by asking God to fill you with the Holy Spirit (Ephesians 5:18). Without the enabling power of the Holy Spirit, you won't have the sustaining power you need to maintain an effective prayer life.

Believe

Belief or faith is the cornerstone of a life based on God's Word. I'll never forget the good example of belief from the Bible—a story your grandfather once shared with me.

The Babylonian king Nebuchadnezzar ordered his guards to throw three men—Shadrach, Meshach, and Abednego—into a "burning fiery furnace" after they refused to bow down to his image.

But before they were thrown into the furnace, the king asked them who they believed could save them. The men answered, " . . . 'O Nebuchadnezzar, we have no need to answer you in this matter. If it be so, our God whom we serve is able to deliver us from the burning fiery furnace; and he will deliver us out of your hand, O king. But if not, be it known to you, O king, that we will not serve your gods or worship the golden image which you have set up" (Daniel 3:16–18, RSV).

The lesson here? They believed that God could save them. More importantly, they believed that God would be with them in the "burning fiery furnace" even if He chose not to save them.

Pray for God's Will

How do you know if your prayers are in God's will? God's Word says: "Thy word is a lamp to my feet and a light to my path" (Psalm 119:105, RSV). If you pray according to God's Word, your prayers are according to His will.

For example, when you pray for someone's salvation, you know you are praying in His will. God desires all men to be saved and to come to the knowledge of the truth (1 Timothy 2:3–4).

And here are some of the other things you can pray for at the start of each day:

- Wisdom (James 1:5)
- Insight and guidance (Proverbs 3:5–6; Isaiah 58:11; Psalm 25:12)
- The Lord's blessing (Jeremiah 17:7–8; Numbers 6:24–26)
- Love (1 Corinthians 13:4–9)
- Joy (Psalm 16:11; John 15:11; 16:24)
- Peace (Isaiah 26:3)
- Protection (Psalm 34:7; 91:11)
- Mercy and grace (Hebrews 4:16)

And for easy reference, list the prayer requests on your smartphone.

Nevertheless, let's remember that even if we do what pleases Him, God may say no to our request. For example, Paul asked God three times to remove a "thorn" in his side. But God told Paul, " . . . My grace is sufficient for you, for my power is made perfect in weakness" (2 Corinthians 12:9, RSV). Remember that it is God's will, not ours.

Pray Specifically

God's Word tells us that if we want something, we need to ask for it *specifically*. This is not a time for generalities.

For example, God's Word tells us that a blind man once realized Jesus was standing near him. The man cried out, " . . . Jesus, Son of David, have mercy on me!" And how did Jesus respond? He said, " . . . What do you want me to do for you?" The blind man said, " . . . Master, let me receive my sight," and Jesus immediately granted his request (Mark 10:47–52, RSV). Note that while the blind man's first request may have garnered Jesus's mercy, it did not result in Jesus granting him sight. The blind man received the miracle of sight only after he made that specific request.

I have a personal example of why it's important to pray in specifics and not in generalities. At one point in our lives, your mother and I were so busy with our respective jobs that we were unable to spend much time together. So I prayed generally to the Lord that He would give us more time to spend together.

And boy, did He answer my prayer. For seven consecutive months, I was with your mother 24/7 as she ran for a statewide office. I should have prayed specifically. I should have said something such as, "Lord, please give me more time to spend with my wife hiking, golfing, and skiing!"

HINDRANCES TO PRAYER

Earlier in the letter, we discussed how some people worry they'll pray the "wrong" way. While *wrong* may be too extreme of a word, it is important to realize that certain decisions, actions, and mind-sets can affect the power and effectiveness of prayer. So just as it's important to discuss the things that can deepen our prayer life, it's also important to address the things that can hinder it.

Unconfessed Sin

God's Word tells us that sin occurs when you know what's the right thing to do but then fail to do it (James 4:17). Bible scholars also define sin as "missing the mark." Using the image of an archer, anything that misses the bull's-eye misses the mark. That is sin.

This analogy is helpful when we try to ignore or minimize our own sin by comparing it with the sin of another person. I often justified my "little white lies" as being acceptable sins because they were not as significant as someone who, for example, committed murder. But my mentor reminded me that God does not grade on a curve. In His eyes, sin is sin. And therefore, we "miss the mark" because even our "acceptable" sins fall short of God's sinless character.

And as stated above, sin hides God's face from you, which means He does not hear your prayer. This is why we discussed above how important it is to confess your sins, so nothing will block you from Him.

Unforgivingness

God wants forgiveness to flow between people as it flows between Him and us. Do you need to forgive anyone? Withholding forgiveness will surely hinder this flow—and hinder your prayers.

Why? Because God's Word tells us, "And whenever you stand praying, forgive, if you have anything against any one; so that your Father also who is in heaven may forgive you your trespasses" (Mark 11:25, RSV).

Lacking Faith

So what exactly is faith? God's Word describes it: "Now faith is the assurance of things hoped for, the conviction of things not seen" (Hebrews 11:1, RSV). In more contemporary terms, faith is a decision-making process and action plan based on the Word of God.

Without faith, it is impossible to please God (Hebrews 11:6). As God's Word tells us, "But let him ask in faith, with no doubting, for he who doubts is like a wave of the sea that is driven and tossed by the wind. For that person must not suppose that a double-minded man, unstable in all his ways, will receive anything from the Lord" (James 1:6–8, RSV).

A Poor Relationship with Your Wife

Being a husband, this one certainly applies to you, son. God's Word tells us that if a married man does not treat his wife well, his prayers will be hindered (1 Peter 3:7). Whether you are a man or a woman, we can extrapolate this message in simple terms: always treat your spouse well.

In fact, God's Word tells husbands to love their spouse as Christ loved the Church and gave up His life for the Church (Ephesians 5:25). Therefore, when a husband sacrificially loves his wife and treats her well, he eliminates a hindrance to prayer.

Asking with an Improper Motive

Earlier, I mentioned that if you're not receiving the things you're praying for, perhaps it means you're asking for the wrong reason. Let's delve deeper into this idea now.

God's Word says, "You ask and do not receive, because you ask wrongly, to spend it on your passions" (James 4:3, RSV). An example is when you're praying to obtain glory for yourself. Glory belongs to God, not to us (Romans 11:36). Martin always told me, "If you touch the glory, you will lose the power."

Before praying, examine your motives. What do you want? Why? As we learned in the fifth letter, ask yourself why at least three times to reach your true reasoning.

All in all, the lessons in these ten letters will guide you in how to live according to God's Word. And by living according to God's Word, you and your family will be in the best possible position to enjoy a happy, successful, and significant life. The more you take these life skills to heart, the more you'll ensure that your motives and prayers will be aligned with God's Word.

THE ONE THING

Here in the tenth letter, you know the drill: now it's time to think of one thing you can do to create and maintain a powerful prayer life.

Maybe for you, the thing is to ask God to search your heart to uncover any unconfessed sin. If there's lingering sin, confess it so it won't hide God's face and hinder your prayer life.

I look forward to your call!

Dad

I push back from the desk. My head and heart are so full. I feel overwhelmed with gratitude for all the information Dad's provided.

I grab my phone and call him.

"Well, son," he says as he answers, "what did you think?"

"Dad, this really *is* the most important life-changing skill! I understand what you mean now.

"I was hoping you would feel that way." I can hear how pleased he is.

Then he pauses. He gives a little clear of his throat.

"Oh man—I almost forgot!" I exclaim. "I bet your friend told you already, but I did a phone interview for that sales job!

I talked with your friend for quite a while. We had great rapport right away. He wants me to come in to meet some of the other team members and have a formal interview in two days. It sounds like a great opportunity with a growing company!"

Dad laughs—proof that he did indeed already know this.

"Ah, wonderful! I'm glad you're excited about it. My friend is too. You'll have to let me know how it goes as things move forward."

"This definitely feels good," I say, beaming. "You know—however it turns out with this job opportunity, I feel like the tide has turned for me. The situation has really changed."

"Well, maybe *you* changed," Dad says wisely.

"For sure—that did occur to me. I'm not feeling so alone. I feel like God's got this. It's not all up to me. I just want to thank you for everything you've taught me during the last ten days, yet saying thank you just isn't enough. But I can't think of any other way to express my gratitude."

"I'm the one that is grateful, son. I can't tell you how happy I am to know that everyone in our entire family is a believer."

"Me, too, Dad."

There's another pause, this time for us both to take in this powerful moment. This is God's love—right here, between us. I don't want this to end, and now I know it doesn't have to.

"Hey," I say after a second or two, "how about I give you a call tomorrow to go over some of the questions I want to ask in the interview? Could you help me with that?"

Dad gives me a big, hearty chuckle. "You know it! Why don't you call about the same time?"

"Great! Then I'll talk to you tomorrow. Thanks again for everything, Dad. I love you!"

"I love you too, son!"

ABOUT THE AUTHOR

Greg Stephens is an attorney and of counsel with Meagher & Geer—one of the country's leading litigation defense and coverage firms. He worked there for forty-three years—twenty-nine years as a trial and litigation attorney and fourteen years as the firm's full-time managing partner.

Since 1981, Greg has been active in Christian ministry as a speaker, teacher, mentor, and writer. He received his Biblical training from the Navigators, a worldwide Christian parachurch organization; from Bible Study Fellowship, an international Christian organization; from his Christian mentor; and from his thirty-eight years of reading, studying, and meditating on God's Word.

Greg resides in Woodbury, Minnesota, with his wife, Mary. They have two adult children, who are married with spouses, and two grandchildren. Greg and Mary attend Eagle Brook Church in Woodbury, Minnesota and Antioch Community Church in Chandler, Arizona.